MW01623250

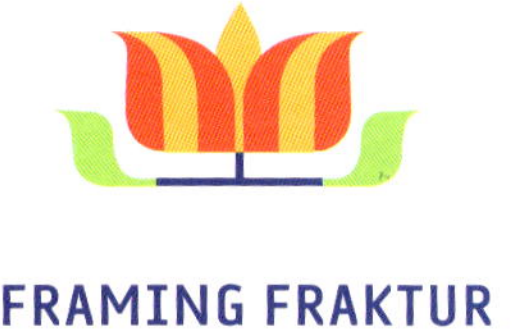

FRAMING FRAKTUR

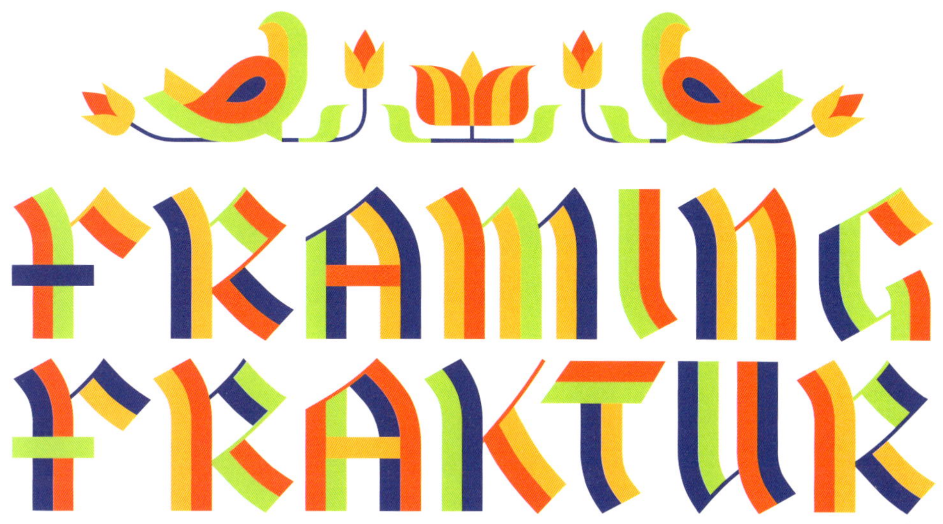

PENNSYLVANIA GERMAN MATERIAL CULTURE & CONTEMPORARY ART

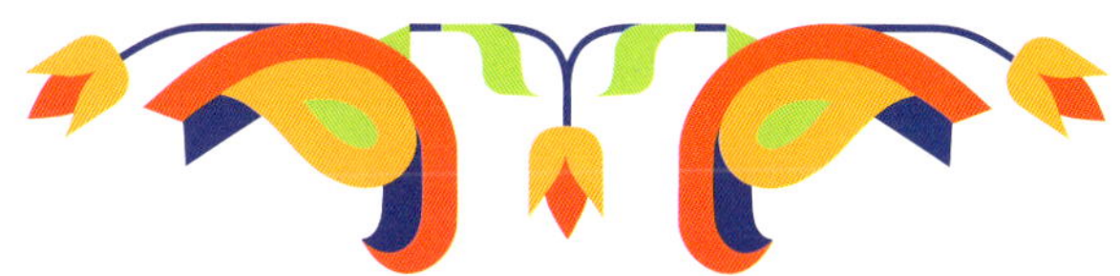

EDITED BY JUDITH TANNENBAUM

FREE LIBRARY OF PHILADELPHIA

DISTRIBUTED BY

UNIVERSITY OF PENNSYLVANIA PRESS

2015

CONTENTS

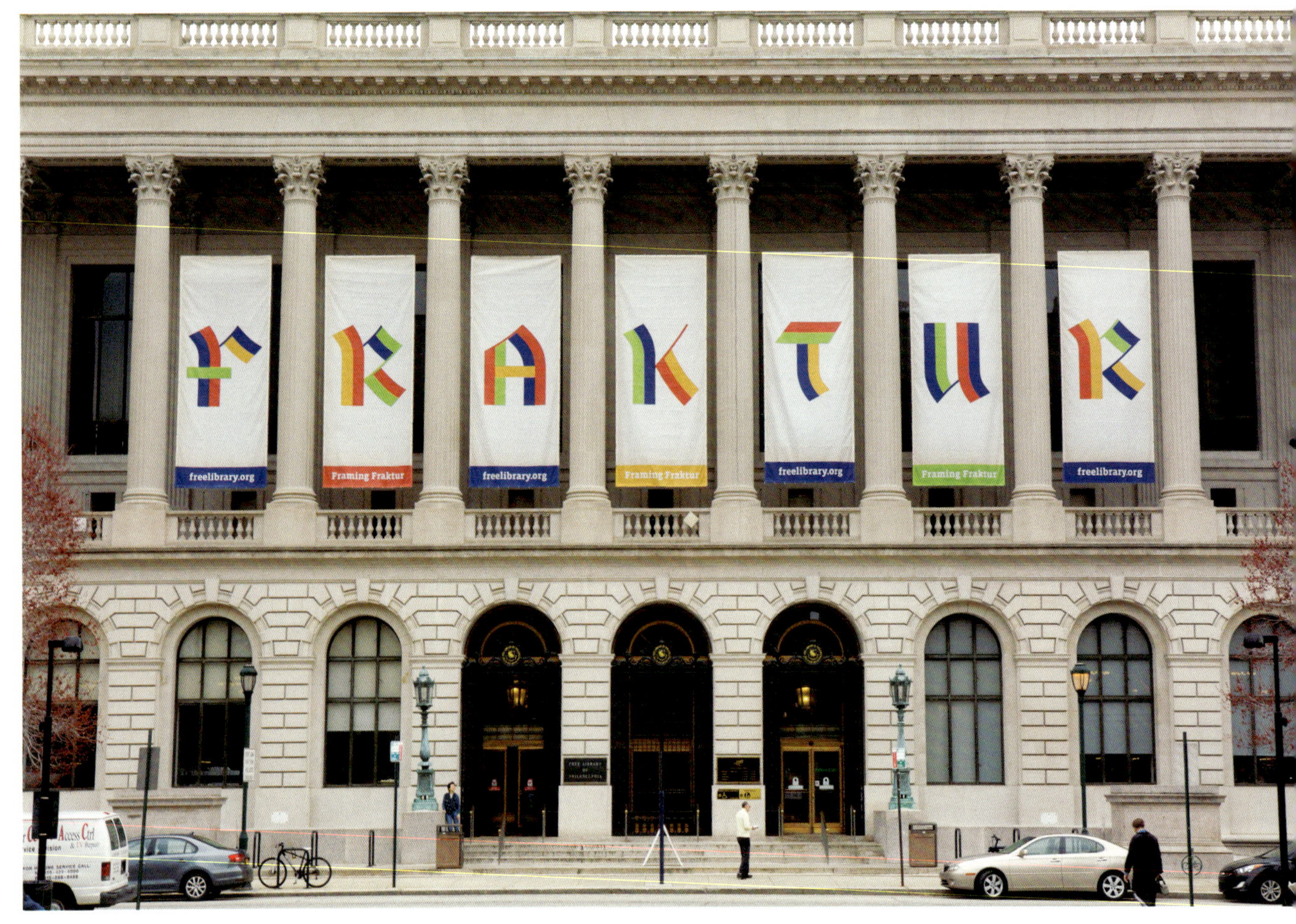

Free Library of Philadelphia,
Parkway Central Library,
1901 Vine Street, with
Framing Fraktur banners.

FOREWORD & ACKNOWLEDGMENTS

The exhibition *Framing Fraktur*, which occasioned the publication of this catalogue, is a very special undertaking for the Free Library of Philadelphia. As the role of libraries is evolving in our twenty-first-century society, the Free Library too is evolving by dramatically changing its approach to public programs. This exhibition is an initial part of that change, and seeks to expand our audience and deepen our engagement with existing audiences by inviting innovative, current interpretation of our historic collections through the work of contemporary artists.

Fraktur is a manuscript-based folk art created by the German immigrants who settled in Pennsylvania beginning in the late seventeenth century. This collaboration with contemporary visual artists to reinterpret and reframe the fraktur collection through a contemporary lens is groundbreaking. While the collection of traditional fraktur at the Free Library is renowned and has been the subject of previous exhibitions and treatises, the mounting of a contemporary art exhibition at the Parkway Central Library is a first. The challenges have been many, but the end result is exciting and exhilarating, as can be seen throughout this book.

The mission of the Free Library of Philadelphia is to advance literacy, guide learning, and inspire curiosity. When we received the grant from The Pew Center for Arts & Heritage (the Center) to mount this ambitious exhibition, it provided the perfect opportunity to combine all aspects of our mission into one. The library as contemporary art museum certainly provided the curiosity factor. In addition to major support from the Center, we are grateful for funding from the Wyeth Foundation for American Art, American Airlines Cargo, Christie's, The Gladys Krieble Delmas Foundation, and the Virginia Cretella Mars Foundation.

Key to the success of the project was enlisting Judith Tannenbaum as curator for the contemporary art exhibition, *Word & Image: Contemporary Artists Connect to Fraktur*. Her wealth of experience enabled her to embark on this adventure with gusto. Likewise, Lisa Minardi brought the same enthusiasm and expertise to the exhibition of traditional fraktur, *Quill & Brush: Pennsylvania German Fraktur and Material Culture*. Their contributions to the exhibition and to this publication are paramount. We are most grateful for their dedication.

None of this would have been possible without the involvement of the contemporary artists, their galleries and staff, and the generosity of individuals who lent artworks to the exhibition. We thank all the artists—Marian Bantjes, Anthony Campuzano, Imran Qureshi, Elaine Reichek, Bob and Roberta Smith, and Gert and Uwe Tobias—for their enthusiastic participation and their extraordinary vision; a number of them created new works specifically for the exhibition. We also thank the following for their assistance and for making work available: Alistair Overbruck (Tobias studio); Paul Kennedy (Reichek studio); Alex Baker and John Ollman, Fleisher/Ollman, Philadelphia; Susan Swenson and Joe Amrhein, Pierogi Gallery, Brooklyn; Tommaso Corvi-Mora, Corvi-Mora, London; Lauren Marinaro and Zach Feuer, Zach Feuer Gallery, New York; Jose Friere and Alissa Bennett, Team Gallery, New York; and Melva Bucksbaum and Raymond Learsy, Ryan Frank, Nicole Klagsbrun, Tamsin Miley, Benjamin Mulvey, and Robert Pfannebecker.

Gratitude must also be extended to Julie Fry, Judy Guston, Josh Harris, Nell McClister, Matthew F. Singer, Paul Trapido, and Jobi Zink. Many members of the Free Library staff must be thanked: Mike Barsanti, Alix Gerz, Amanda Goldstein, Melissa Greenberg, Sandy Horrocks, Rachel Karasick, Karen Lightner, Jim Pecora, Janine Pollock, and Donald Root, as well as the staff of Collection Care and the Rare Book Department. All contributed greatly to the success of the project.

—*Siobhan A. Reardon, President and Director, The Free Library of Philadelphia*

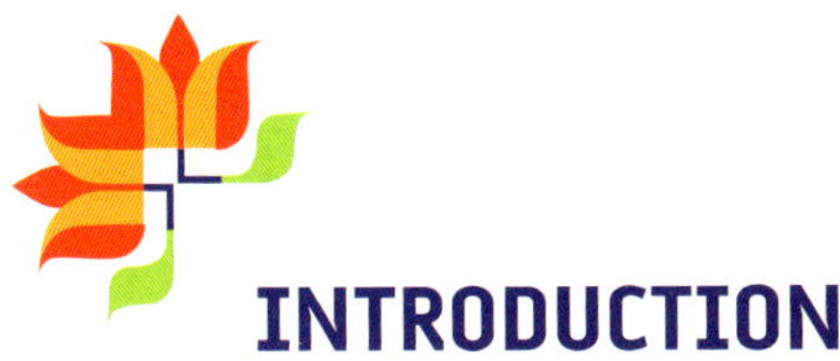

INTRODUCTION

Pennsylvania German fraktur and contemporary art might sound like odd bedfellows. How did the Free Library of Philadelphia come to connect these two very different types of art—a centuries-old folk genre and the esoteric visual art of today—and what was the impetus to do so?

Type designers and graphic designers are familiar with so-called blackletter typefaces known as *Fraktur* or the "German alphabet," which dates back to the sixteenth century but was still commonly used in German-speaking and other Northern European countries in the early twentieth century. In *Fraktur* lettering, lines are broken up ("fractured"), and forms are angular—in contrast to the curves of other common Northern European typefaces that use the Latin alphabet. *Fraktur* script or lettering is prominent in Pennsylvania German decorated documents—birth and baptismal certificates, writing samples, religious texts, and other documents in which decorative motifs such as tulips, hearts, and angels accompany elaborate script. These documents themselves started to be referred to as fraktur in the late nineteenth century after Henry Chapman Mercer (1856–1930), an American archeologist, historian, collector, tile-maker, and designer from Doylestown, Pennsylvania, described the "art of Fractur" in a speech given to and published by the American Philosophical Society in 1897.

The idea for this exhibition grew out of conversations between staff of the Free Library, which has a large and significant collection of fraktur documents, books, and related objects, and staff of The Pew Center for Arts & Heritage, which, among its various programs, supports exhibitions that challenge boundaries and break new ground. The library decided to propose a two-part exhibition, *Framing Fraktur*, that would showcase the work of artists for whom the use of written language is integrally tied to visual imagery and who may also riff on folk genres. The idea was not to trace a direct inspiration from fraktur, but to identify an underlying resonance between the eighteenth- and nineteenth-century documents housed in the Rare Book Department and the approach or interests of the contemporary artists.

Gert and Uwe Tobias, identical twins who live and work in Cologne, Germany, were the first artists identified for *Word & Image: Contemporary Artists Connect to Fraktur*. The Tobias brothers were born in Brasov, Romania, in the Transylvanian region of the country, but they belong to a German-speaking minority group known as *Siebenbürger Sachsen* (Transylvanian Saxons). At the age of twelve, they moved to Germany with their family. They are now recognized internationally for their unusually large woodblock prints, which incorporate rich folkloric traditions of their native land and handicrafts associated with their ethnic identity merged with a deep knowledge of modern art and design (Russian Constructivism, geometric abstraction, and Surrealism).

Because of its impressive scale, the Tobiases' work was designated for the grand lobby of the Free Library's Neoclassical building, where everyone walking in the door would encounter it. Five other artists who work in a wide variety of styles and with diverse subject matter would be showcased in different areas of the first and second floors. Marian Bantjes, from Vancouver, started her career as a type designer but has branched out into florid drawings and a wonderfully witty and concise writing style. Anthony Campuzano, from Philadelphia, adapts texts from newspaper headlines, songs, and personal notes that become colorful, obsessively marked, patterned grounds. Imran Qureshi, who lives in Lahore, Pakistan, was trained in traditional Mughal manuscript painting and is known for subtly layered compositions that reflect on current events and personal experiences in his turbulent country. Elaine Reichek, a lifelong New Yorker, is recognized for her distinctive embroidered samplers—a traditional folk genre once practiced by girls and young women—into which she introduces ancient myths, Western art and literature, and popular culture from her vantage point as a woman belonging to a particular time and culture. Bob and Roberta Smith (a.k.a. Patrick Brill), a British artist known for sign paintings made with found materials in the tradition of placards and broadsides, has become a modern-day campaigner and activist for art and art education.

The relationship of these artists' works to fraktur is considered in greater depth in my essay in this catalogue, "Connecting Present to Past: Contemporary Artists with Links to Fraktur." The history of fraktur and how the documents were collected as well as current scholarship about representative examples and their categorization are the subjects of essays by Janine Pollock and Lisa Minardi, the curator of *Quill & Brush: Pennsylvania German Fraktur and Material Culture*, the concurrent exhibition of traditional fraktur in the library's Rare Book Department. Taking a broad view, Matthew F. Singer considers fraktur's historical context in relation to modern and contemporary art movements spanning from Cubism and Dada to graffiti and street art.

Framing Fraktur has several goals: to introduce art into the daily lives of library visitors; to acquaint people with the extraordinary resources of the Rare Book Department; to raise awareness of fraktur, an art form with particular significance for the southeastern Pennsylvania region; to connect the art and literature of past and present; and to bring the work of seven contemporary artists to a large and diverse audience. With the technological advances of recent years, libraries are undergoing major changes and reevaluating what they can and should be in order to serve their communities. Projects like *Framing Fraktur* extend the definition of what a library is today and pose questions about what it can be in the future. The sky's the limit.

—Judith Tannenbaum, Consulting Curator

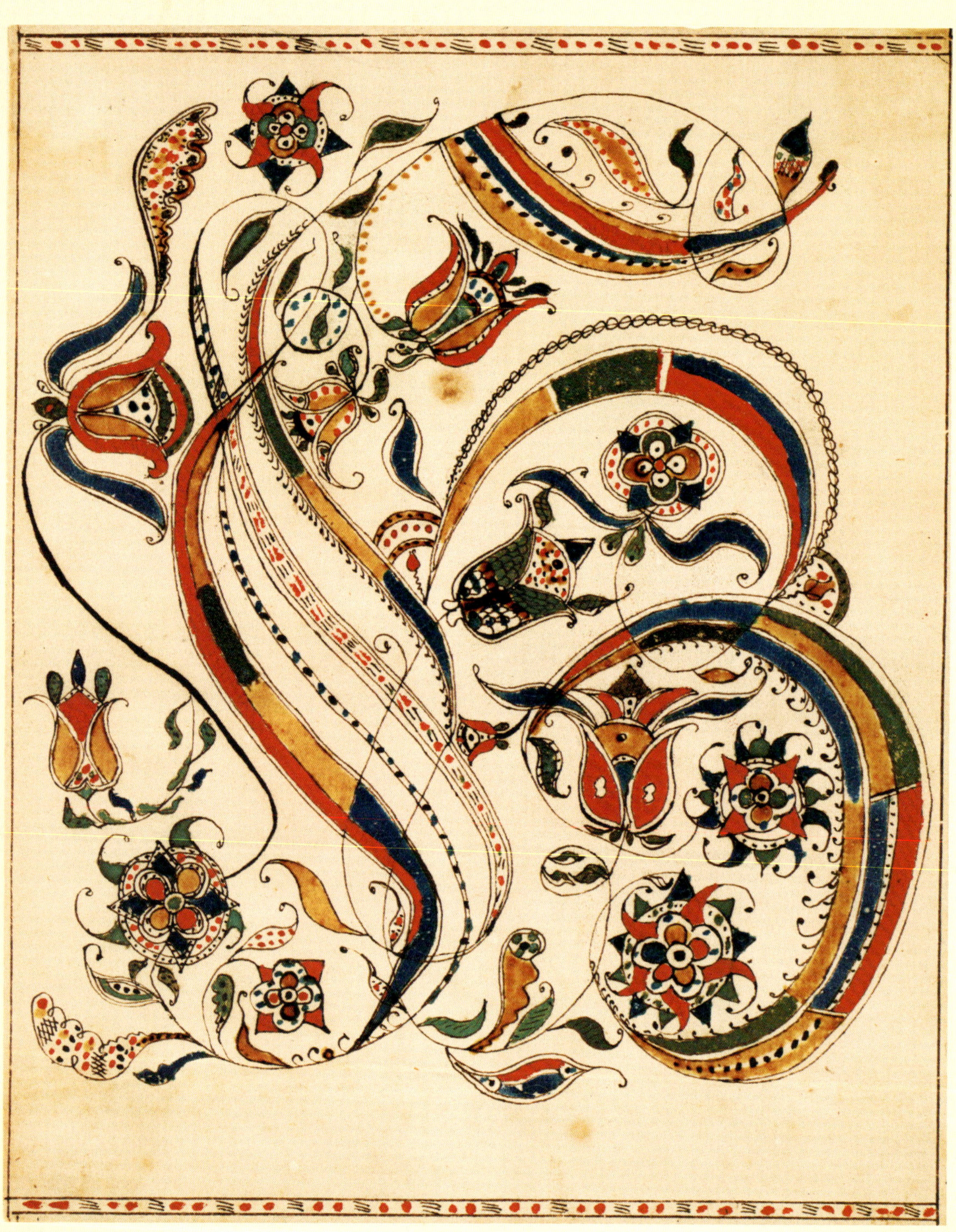

JANINE POLLOCK

THE FREE LIBRARY OF PHILADELPHIA'S PENNSYLVANIA GERMAN COLLECTION

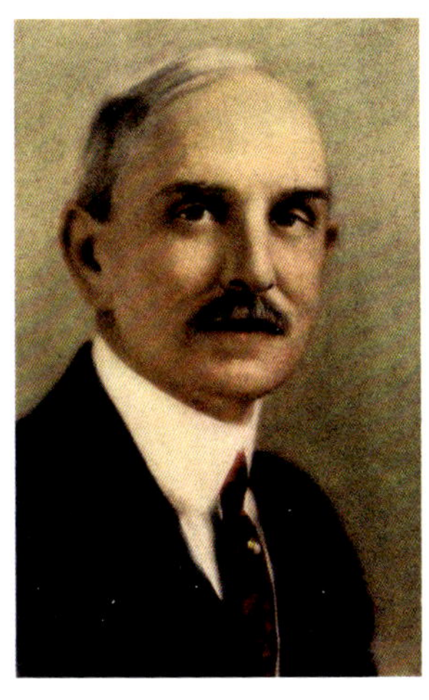

FIG. 1 (LEFT)
Letter H. Attributed to Susanna Heebner (1750–1818), Worcester Township, Montgomery County, Pennsylvania, c. 1810. Watercolor and ink on laid paper, 8¼ x 6⅝ in.
FREE LIBRARY OF PHILADELPHIA

FIG. 2 (ABOVE)
Henry Stauffer Borneman. Photographic reproduction after original painting.
FREE LIBRARY OF PHILADELPHIA, RARE BOOK DEPARTMENT, DONOR FILE

The Free Library of Philadelphia's outstanding Pennsylvania German Collection is the culmination of the life's work of four major collectors and the passionate dedication of two of my esteemed predecessors in the Rare Book Department. Through a remarkable convergence of events in the late 1950s, the Free Library became home to one of the largest collections of fraktur in a public institution (fig. 1).[1]

Over the course of his eighty-four years, the visionary collector Henry Stauffer Borneman (1870–1955; fig. 2) amassed a vast and unprecedentedly comprehensive collection: books representing the earliest German printing in America; handwritten music, weaving, accounting, and prayer books; and the beautifully decorated *Frakturschriften*.[2] Borneman, who was the founder and first dean of Temple University's School of Law, was of Pennsylvania German ancestry. As a young man he became keenly interested in preserving the books and manuscripts so closely associated with his heritage. His first fraktur was given to him by his grandmother.[3]

Borneman was a knowledgeable collector and a pioneer in fraktur research who wrote important books and articles on fraktur and Pennsylvania German culture.[4] He was president of the Pennsylvania German Society for many years. In October of 1952 Borneman lent some of the items in his collection to the Free Library for an exhibition and gave a talk at the library about fraktur (fig. 3).

Borneman's collecting interests were wide and varied—from a first edition of *Leaves of Grass* to medieval manuscripts to modern fine-press books—but he was most devoted to the study of the cultural contribution of Germans to Pennsylvania, particularly in the realm of folk art in

THE FREE LIBRARY OF PHILADELPHIA
LOGAN SQUARE — PARKWAY AT 19th STREET

YOU ARE CORDIALLY INVITED TO HEAR A TALK BY HENRY S. BORNEMAN, ESQ., ON

FRAKTUR—SCHRIFTEN

The art of illumination as practiced by the Pennsylvania Germans popularly known as the Pennsylvania Dutch

FRIDAY, OCTOBER 25, AT 8:30 P. M.
THE LECTURE HALL OF THE FREE LIBRARY

Mr. Borneman's remarkable Collection of Pennsylvania German Illuminated Manuscripts and Books is on display at the Free Library during October.

COME AND BRING YOUR FRIENDS
ADMISSION FREE — NO TICKETS REQUIRED

FIG. 3
Invitation to a lecture by Henry S. Borneman in the Rare Book Department, October 25, 1952.
FREE LIBRARY OF PHILADELPHIA, RARE BOOK DEPARTMENT, DONOR FILE

fraktur, manuscripts, and printed books.[5] When Borneman died, in 1955, his family hired the Philadelphia book dealer Charles Sessler to handle the sale of the collection. Moncure Biddle, a member of the Free Library of Philadelphia's board of trustees, learned of the sale and informed Ellen Shaffer, then Rare Book Librarian. Shaffer was very interested, as the subject matter complemented the department's stellar collection of early Americana and had such a profound local connection. Biddle was able to arrange for the sale using library trust funds. It was the first time a collection had been purchased by, rather than gifted to, the library and was the largest acquisition through purchase in its history, according to the library's then-president, Emerson Greenaway.

The German-speaking immigrants to America, who began arriving in Philadelphia in 1683, brought with them a strong work ethic, a love of education, and devout religious beliefs, all of which were represented in Borneman's collection. The collection contained 400 fraktur, 160 fraktur bookplates, and 700 books and manuscripts. Included in the sale was the first Bible printed in a European language in the western hemisphere, printed in 1743 by Christopher Saur Sr. in Germantown. In the collection could be found examples of most types of fraktur. The collection also contained a fraktur artist's case, with bottles for ink, verses written

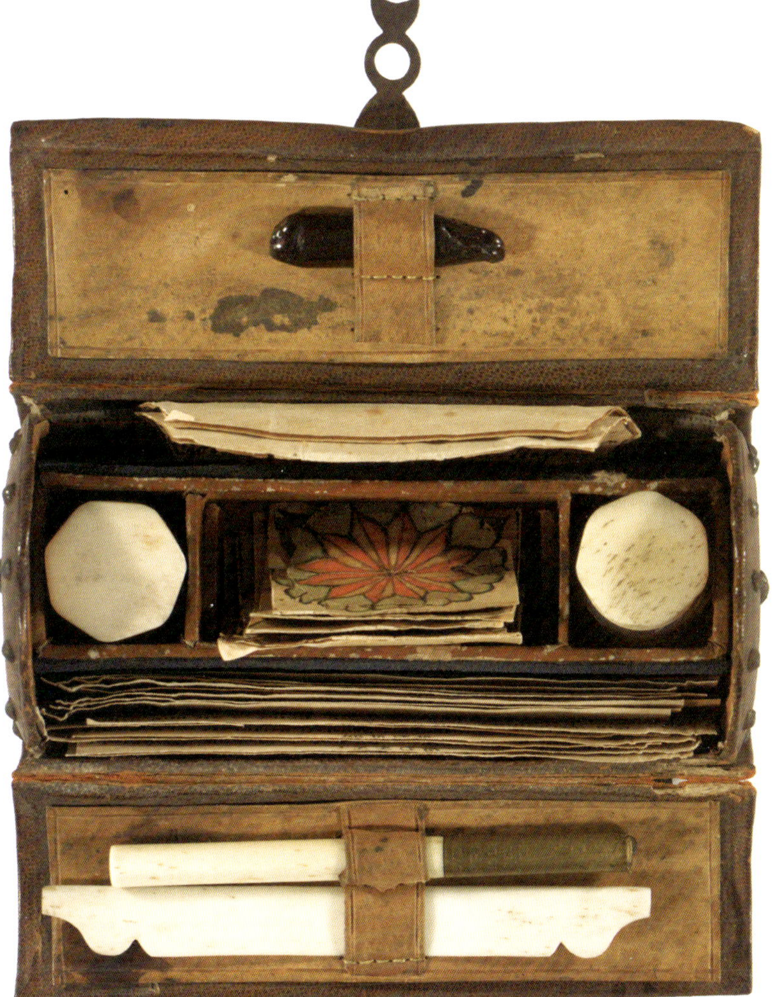

FIG. 4
Fraktur artist's toolkit. Southeastern Pennsylvania, c. 1800. This leather case holds a straightedge, two glass containers with bone lids for ink and sand (pounce), and other implements used to write and make decorated manuscripts.
FREE LIBRARY OF PHILADELPHIA

in script, and samples of designs that are attributable to the Wetzel Geometric Artist (fig. 4).

Opportunities to enhance the collection soon followed. Shaffer, who led most of the efforts to purchase fraktur as they came available, could not have been more pleased at the collection she was stewarding. In a 1955 letter to Mabel Zahn of the Charles Sessler firm, Shaffer declares, "I am more than happy over the collection and I think it is going to do a lot for the Free Library to have it here."[6] Shaffer saw to this herself by writing articles describing the glories of the library's fraktur for publications like *Pennsylvania Folk Life*, *Manuscripts*, and the *Graphic Arts Review*.

Shaffer's efforts quickly paid off. The collection of the antiques dealer Levi E. Yoder, consisting of 275 fraktur and fraktur bookplates, was made

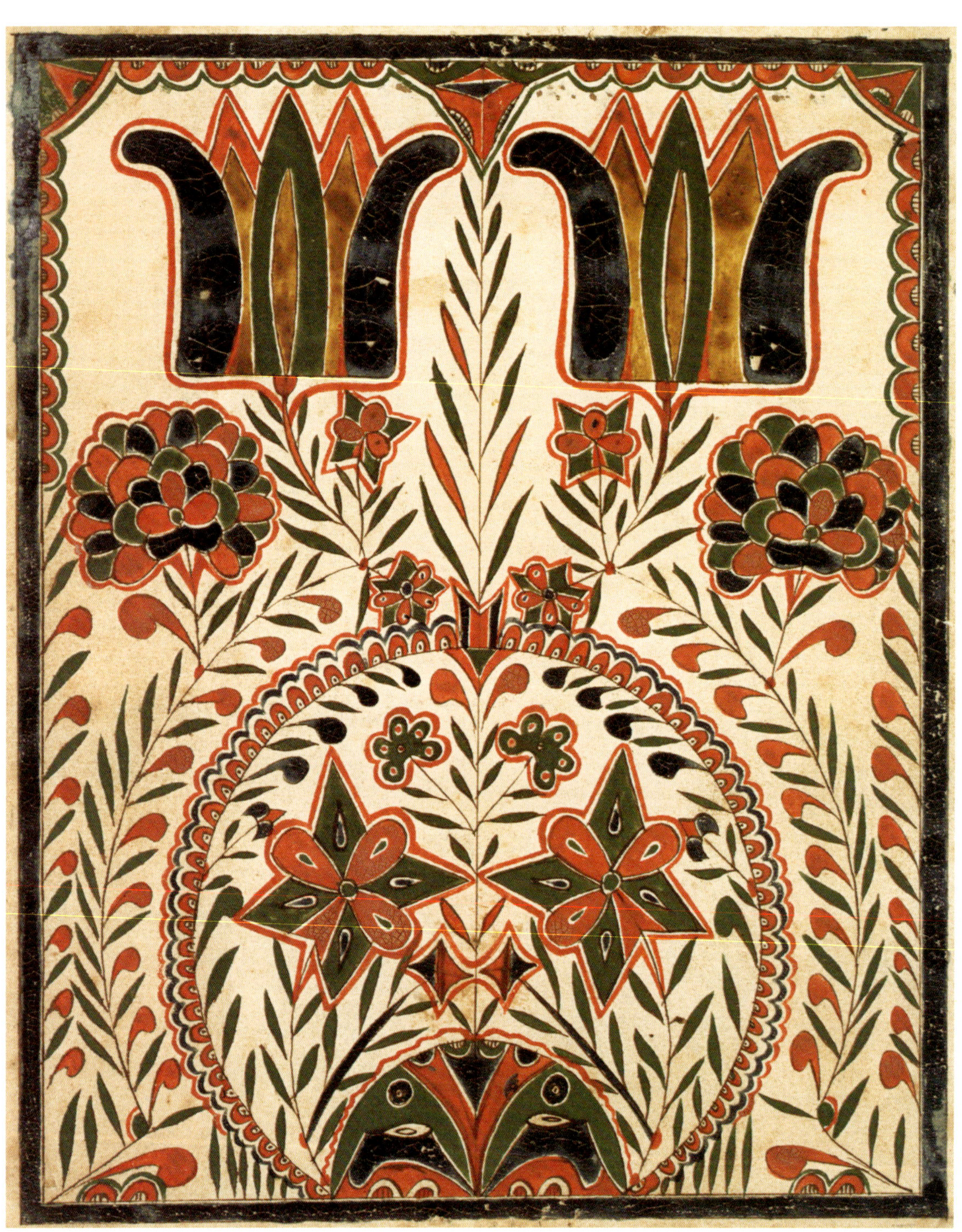

FIG. 5 (LEFT)
Reward of merit (drawing of flowers). Southeastern Pennsylvania, c. 1820. Watercolor and ink on wove paper, 7⅝ x 6⅜ in.
FREE LIBRARY OF PHILADELPHIA

FIG. 6 (BELOW)
Woodblock. Northampton-Lehigh County, Pennsylvania, c. 1800. Pine, 13⅛ x 15 x 1 in. It is unclear what the purpose of the woodblock was, as it does not appear to have been heavily used. Perhaps it helped the artist mark the outline of his design before he finalized it with ink and watercolor.
FREE LIBRARY OF PHILADELPHIA

available to the Free Library for purchase upon his death in 1957. In his forty-four years in business in Silverdale, Bucks County, Yoder had taken advantage of his prime location in fraktur country to add to his personal collection all the fraktur that came his way. In fact, the only fraktur he ever sold were a few to Henry Borneman.[7] Two examples of important items from this collection are a large, colorful drawing of flowers in pristine condition (fig. 5) and a carved woodblock, possibly used by the Flying Angel Artist (active c. 1780–1811) to print fraktur (fig. 6).

Language teacher Wilbur H. Oda was a collector of early German American language imprints who in retirement began work on a bibliography of them. Upon Oda's untimely death the collection was made available to the library for purchase. The group of 600 imprints added 13 centers of early German printing in America to the 41 already represented in the library's collection.[8]

L. B. Kuhn was a chemical engineer by training who also collected early German American imprints. He was a friend of Dr. Oda who was waiting in great anticipation for the forthcoming bibliography. After

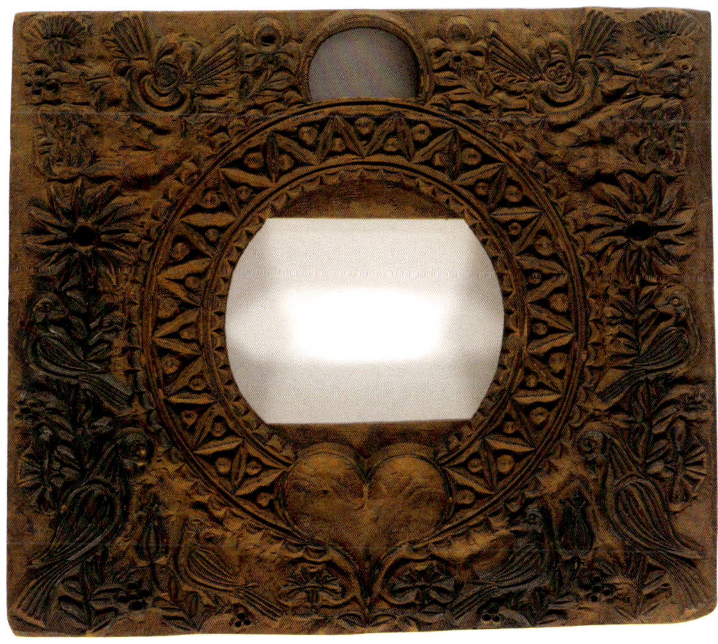

Oda died, Kuhn attempted to carry on the work. In 1956 he contacted Howell Heaney, who was at that time bibliographer in the Rare Book Department. In a letter Kuhn confessed to Heaney that he did not have the training required for the undertaking but included for Heaney's critical review a sample of the collation statements he was creating.[9] Heaney kindly assured Kuhn that he was on the right track and that he need only be consistent and explain his methodology in the introduction. Heaney closed by saying how much he was looking forward to the completed work and asking, "Can't you come down to Philadelphia one day so that we can have a good talk?" letting Kuhn know that even a Saturday or Sunday would be fine and offering to give directions to his home.[10]

These letters were the beginning of a relationship well documented in the Rare Book Department's correspondence files. In December of the same year Kuhn wrote to say he had given up on the bibliography and was selling his collection of 400 imprints. In February of 1957 Heaney and Shaffer visited the Kuhns at their Douglasville, Pennsylvania, home and selected 200 of the 400 volumes for purchase. When they returned a few weeks later to pick up the books, cardboard boxes in hand, L. B.'s wife, Janet, served lunch, and Heaney and Shaffer enjoyed getting to know the children. At the conclusion of their transaction Shaffer wrote to the Kuhns on behalf of herself and Heaney, "I don't think either of us ever bought books under more pleasant circumstances."[11]

The warm and friendly letters between the librarians and the collectors reveal a subtle strategy whereby Shaffer and Heaney made their desires known and were always welcoming and more than accommodating, connecting with the collector on a deeply personal level, while shrewdly bargaining to get the books they want for the price they want. In less than three years Shaffer and Heaney had staked out the library's position as the major center for Pennsylvania German holdings. The collection became so well known that in 1958 four of the library's fraktur were selected by the State Department to represent the state of Pennsylvania at the "Face of America" exhibit at the World's Fair in Brussels (fig. 7).

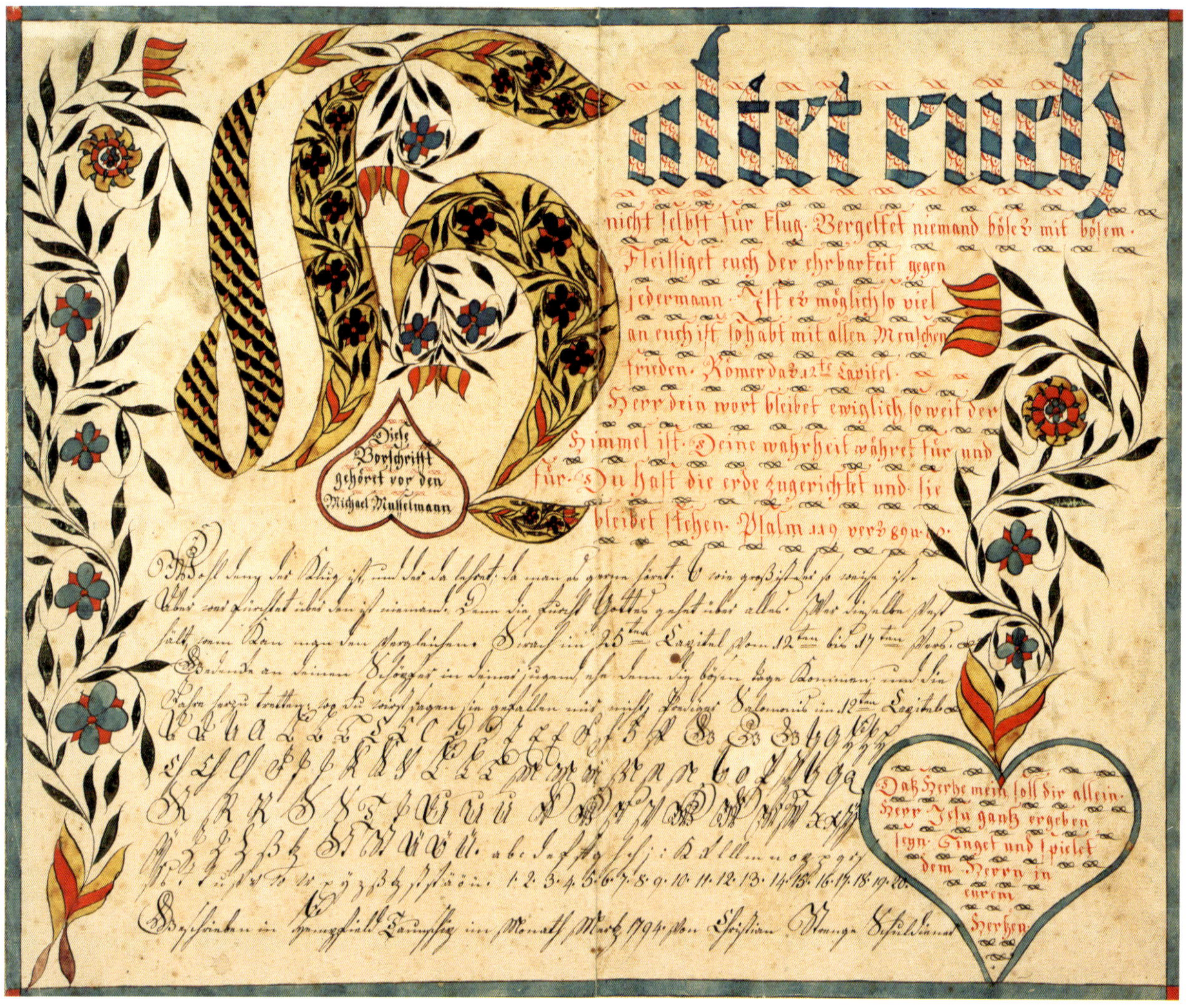

FIG. 7

Writing sample for Michael Musselmann. Christian Strenge, Hempfield Township, Lancaster County, Pennsylvania, 1794. Watercolor and ink on laid paper, 12⅝ x 15⅜ in. This fraktur was one of four from the Free Library of Philadelphia collection that were shown in the "Face of America" exhibit at the 1958 World's Fair in Brussels.

FREE LIBRARY OF PHILADELPHIA

The growing holdings brought more collectors and scholars to the Rare Book Department's door. Pastor Frederick S. Weiser was an expert in Pennsylvania German culture who wrote books and articles on the topic and became a major collector of fraktur. He was captivated by the Free Library's collection, using it as a resource for his scholarship as well as offering some of his fraktur, manuscripts, and imprints to the department at cost. After Shaffer had moved on and Heaney retired, Weiser continued to offer items to their successors. In 1984 one fraktur in particular from Maryland was rejected by the librarian, in the hopes that another would turn up in better condition. With understated incredulity Weiser wrote, "I was sorry you did not take the Frederick County one. I have never seen it before and since it was an area in which they were buried with the people, I doubt another one like it is around."[12]

Pastor Weiser spoke from a deep knowledge of the department's fraktur holdings. In 1976 Weiser and Heaney compiled most of the Free Library's fraktur into a publication, *The Pennsylvania German Fraktur of the Free Library of Philadelphia: An Illustrated Catalogue.*[13] This groundbreaking two-volume set was published by the Pennsylvania German Society, presenting valuable research along with images and translations of more than 1,000 fraktur. The affection and esteem among Shaffer, Heaney, and Weiser is palpable in the Rare Book Department's correspondence files (fig. 8) as well as in the collection itself: in 1995 Weiser donated seven broadsides to the collection in memory of Ellen Shaffer, who had passed away the previous year.

More recent developments have brought the collection to the attention of genealogists, collectors, and scholars throughout the world. In 2007 the Free Library received funding from the Barra Foundation to digitize the fraktur collection. This two-year project consisted of scanning the fraktur at high resolution and transcribing, translating, and cataloging them in a comprehensive database. This fully searchable database indexes owners, makers, types of fraktur, media, techniques, and locale. In addition it is searchable by surname via the Soundex system used by the United States Census Bureau. In 2011 the library received a

FIG. 8

Postcard from Frederick Weiser to Howell Heaney, postmarked October 15, 1975. "We saw a wonderful exhibition in Basel and in Strasbourg of *Taufscheine + Vorschriften*. A few would have stumped this expert. Shades of the Geometric Wetzel artist on the reverse!"

FREE LIBRARY OF PHILADELPHIA, RARE BOOK DEPARTMENT, CORRESPONDENCE FILE

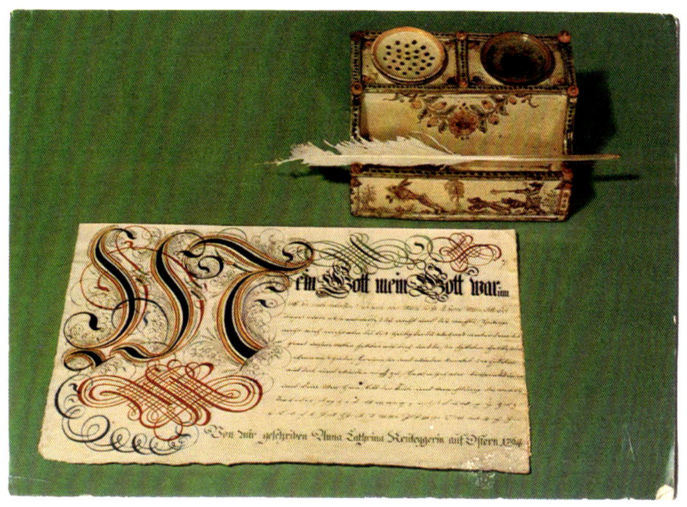

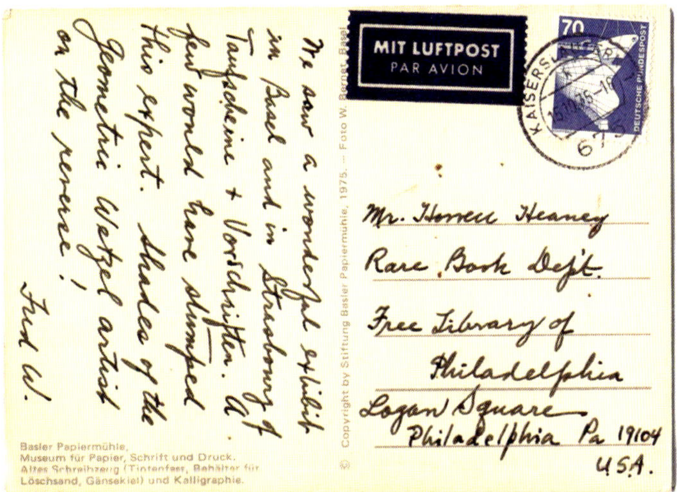

grant from the National Endowment of the Humanities through its Save America's Treasures Program to conserve the 171 manuscripts in the collection.

George Eckhardt, who knew the collection during Borneman's lifetime and wrote a 1957 article about it for *The Magazine Antiques* (fig. 9), said it would take years of research to comprehend what it contains,

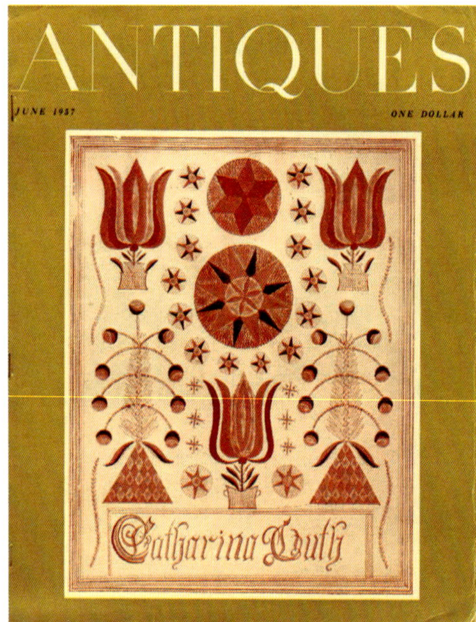

FIG. 9
Cover of *The Magazine Antiques*, June 1957, with an article on the Free Library's Pennsylvania German Collection by George Eckhardt.
FREE LIBRARY OF PHILADELPHIA, RARE BOOK DEPARTMENT, CURATORIAL FILE

and "the institution fortunate enough to have it will be a focal point in Pennsylvania German history and research."[14] Exhibitions like *Framing Fraktur*, along with programs and conferences at the library, aim to ensure the accuracy of this prediction.

NOTES

1 The Schwenkfelder Library & Heritage Center in Pennsburg, Pennsylvania, has more than 1,000 fraktur in its collection. The Newberry Library in Chicago owns more than 1,000 printed birth and baptismal certificates, previously in the collection of Klaus Stopp.

2 Ellen Shaffer, Rare Book Department librarian from 1955 to 1970, called Borneman's collection at the time "the most comprehensive collection of Pennsylvania German material ever assembled." Ellen Shaffer, "H. S. Borneman Collection Acquired by Free Library," *Graphic Arts Review* vol. xviii, no. 10 (October 1955).

3 Frances Lichten, *Fraktur: The Illuminated Manuscripts of the Pennsylvania Dutch* (Philadelphia: Free Library of Philadelphia, 1958).

4 See Henry S. Borneman, *Pennsylvania German Illuminated Manuscripts: A Classification of Fraktur-Schriften and an Inquiry into their History and Art* (Norristown, PA: Pennsylvania German Society, 1938). This landmark publication outlines a classification system that organized fraktur based on the document's function, a system

the Free Library still uses to organize its fraktur, including in the online database. This book also served as the initial catalog of Borneman's fraktur collection. See also Henry S. Borneman, *Pennsylvania German Bookplates: A Study* (Philadelphia: Pennsylvania German Society, 1953).

5 George R. Staab, "Noted Lawyer's Collection of Books, Papers to Be Sold," *The Sunday Bulletin* (October 23, 1955). Henry Borneman's obituary details the breadth of his collection: "The books and other items he bought faithfully reflected keen preoccupation with the finest in literature, the part played in American history by the early German settlers, and the beginnings of Christianity."

6 Letter from Ellen Shaffer to Mabel Zahn, June 28, 1955. Correspondence files of the Rare Book Department of the Free Library of Philadelphia.

7 Ellen Shaffer, "Illuminators, Scribes and Printers: A Glimpse of the Free Library's Pennsylvania Dutch Collection," *Pennsylvania Folklife* vol. 9, no. 4 (Fall 1958): 18–27.

8 Ibid.

9 Letter from L. B. Kuhn to Howell Heaney, May 1, 1956. Correspondence files of the Rare Book Department of the Free Library of Philadelphia.

10 Letter from Howell Heaney to L. B. Kuhn, May 3, 1956. Correspondence files of the Rare Book Department of the Free Library of Philadelphia.

11 Letter from Ellen Shaffer to L. B. and Janet Kuhn, March 6, 1957. Correspondence files of the Rare Book Department of the Free Library of Philadelphia.

12 Letter from Pastor Frederick Weiser to Frank Halpern, February 28, 1984. Correspondence files of the Rare Book Department of the Free Library of Philadelphia.

13 Frederick S. Weiser and Howell J. Heaney, *The Pennsylvania German Fraktur of the Free Library of Philadelphia: An Illustrated Catalogue*, 2 vols. (Breinigsville, PA: Pennsylvania German Society, 1976).

14 George H. Eckhardt, "The Henry S. Borneman Collection of Pennsylvania German Fracturs," *The Magazine Antiques* (June 1957): 538–40.

Janine Pollock is assistant chief of the Central Public Services Division of the Free Library of Philadelphia. In her previous position as head of the Free Library's Rare Book Department, she presided over exhibitions on topics including William Shakespeare, Charles Dickens, Early Americana, and Pennsylvania German fraktur.

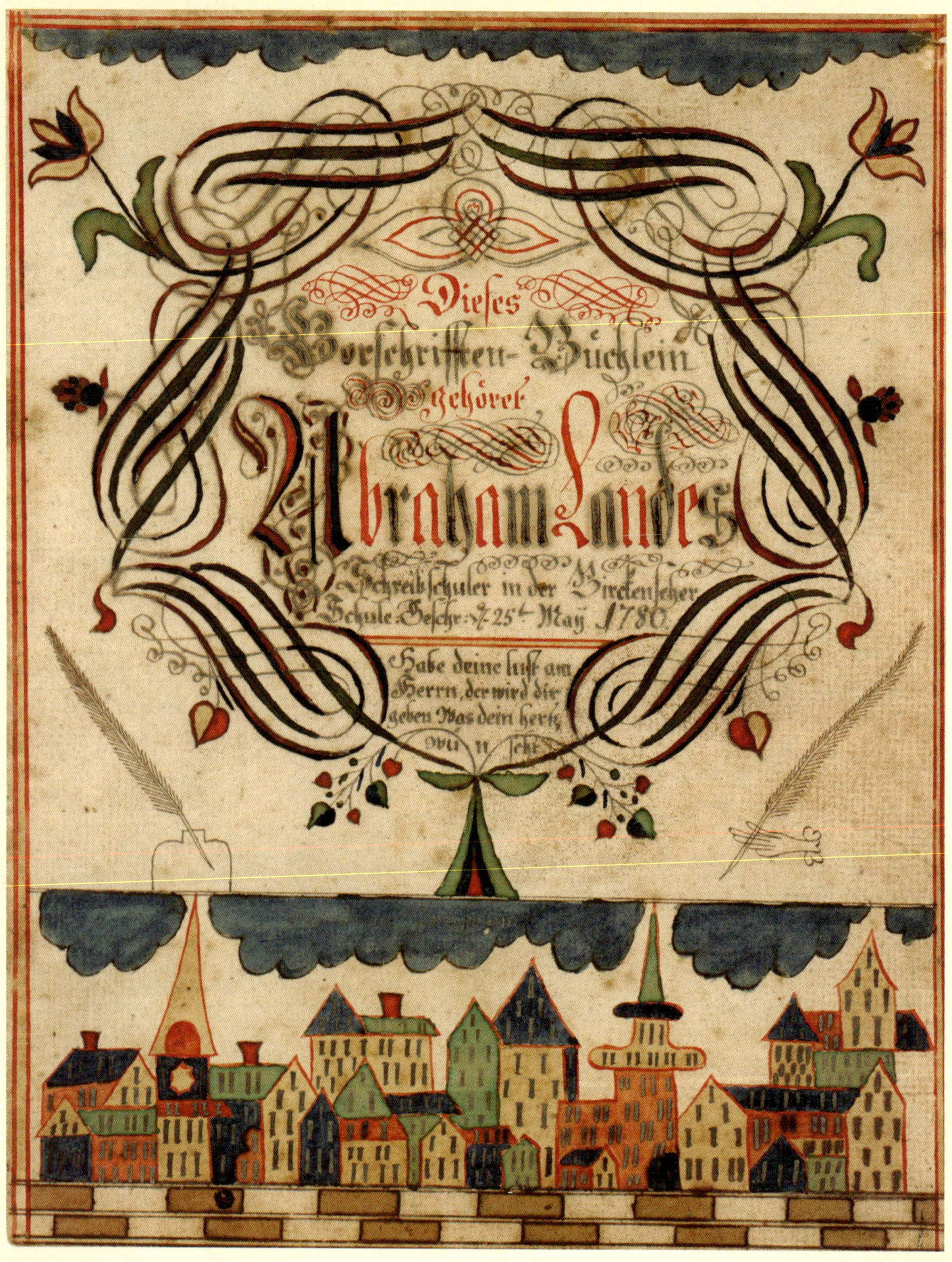
Dieses
Vorschriften-Büchlein
gehöret
Abraham Landes
Schreibschuler in der Birckenseher
Schule. Geschr: d. 25th May 1780.
Habe deine lust am
Herrn, der wird dir
geben was dein hertz
wu n sche

LISA MINARDI

QUILL & BRUSH: AN INTRODUCTION TO PENNSYLVANIA GERMAN FRAKTUR

FIG. 10 (LEFT)
Writing sample booklet with bookplate for Abraham Landes. Attributed to Johann Adam Eyer (1755–1837), Perkasie School, Hilltown Township, Bucks County, Pennsylvania, May 25, 1780. Watercolor and ink on laid paper, 8⅜ x 6⅞ in. This bookplate was made for a writing sample booklet, or *Vorschriften Büchlein*, based on Swiss prototypes. A typical example consists of four pages—including hymns, biblical verses, and alphabets—and an ornate bookplate.
FREE LIBRARY OF PHILADELPHIA

The Free Library of Philadelphia is home to an extraordinary collection of Pennsylvania German fraktur (decorated manuscripts and printed documents), books, ephemera, and related artifacts (fig. 10). Established in 1955 with the acquisition of more than 600 fraktur from the estate of Philadelphia attorney Henry S. Borneman, the collection now totals more than 1,300 pieces and is one of the largest holdings in the country. This essay provides an overview of Pennsylvania German fraktur, beginning with a brief look at the people who made and owned these remarkable documents, followed by highlights from the Free Library collection.

THE PENNSYLVANIA GERMANS

Beginning in 1683 with the founding of Germantown and continuing through 1775, approximately 80,000 German-speaking immigrants settled in southeastern Pennsylvania. Now known as the Pennsylvania Germans (or Pennsylvania Dutch), this population was diverse in its European origins and religious beliefs. Approximately 90 percent were from the Palatinate region of southwest Germany and belonged to the Lutheran or German Reformed Church. The remaining 10 percent included the Amish and Mennonites, largely from the German-speaking cantons of Switzerland; Schwenkfelders, from Silesia (part of modern-day Poland); Moravians, primarily from Bohemia and Moravia; Catholics; and Jews. By 1790 German-speaking people constituted about 40 percent of the population in southeastern Pennsylvania. Most lived in the counties of Berks, Lancaster, Lebanon, Lehigh, Montgomery, Northampton, Northumberland, and York. Philadelphia was also home to a sizable number of Germans. In 1800, people of German heritage vied with those of English ancestry as the largest ethnic group in the city, with both populations estimated at 32 to 35 percent of the total 68,000 residents. Wherever these German-speaking immigrants settled, their distinctive material culture traditions—especially fraktur—flourished.[1]

MAKING FRAKTUR

Fraktur is a Germanic tradition of decorating manuscripts and printed documents that was transplanted to Pennsylvania by German-speaking immigrants. The term is derived from the Latin *fractura* (breaking) and refers to the broken or fractured style of lettering known in German as *Fraktur* (see fig. 68). During the 1900s, the art form came to be referred to by the anglicized term "fraktur." In Pennsylvania, the most common type of fraktur was the *Geburts-und-Taufschein*, or birth and baptismal certificate. Less common were marriage certificates and death memorials.

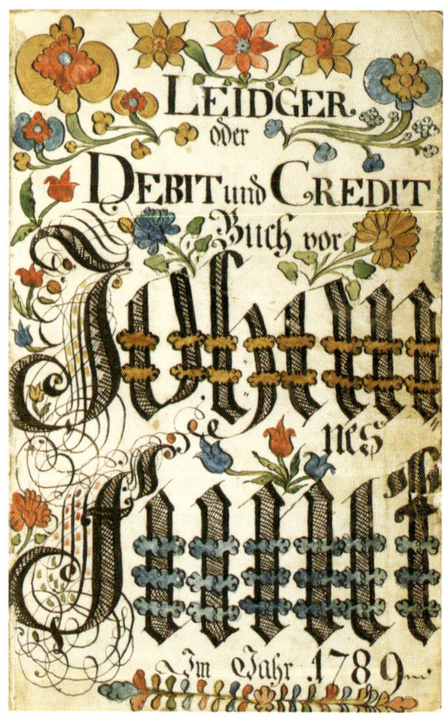

FIG. 11
Account book with bookplate for Johannes Funck. Attributed to Johannes Ernst Spangenberg (c. 1755–1814), Northampton County, Pennsylvania, 1789. Watercolor and ink on laid paper, $12\frac{3}{8} \times 7\frac{3}{4}$ in. Formerly known as the Easton Bible Artist, Spangenberg was one of the most accomplished fraktur artists working in the Lehigh-Northampton County region.
FREE LIBRARY OF PHILADELPHIA

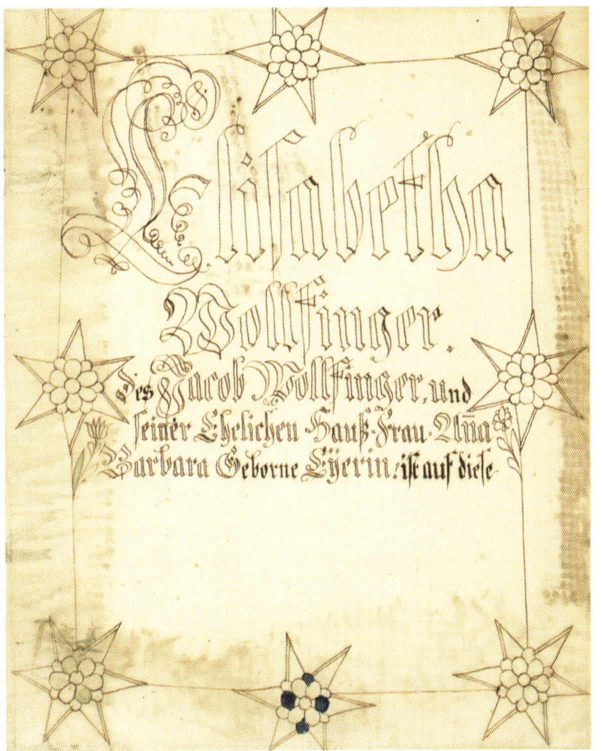
Elisabetha
Wollfinger.
Des Jacob Wollfinger, und
seiner Ehelichen Hauß-Frau Aña
Barbara Geborne Eyerin, ist auf diese

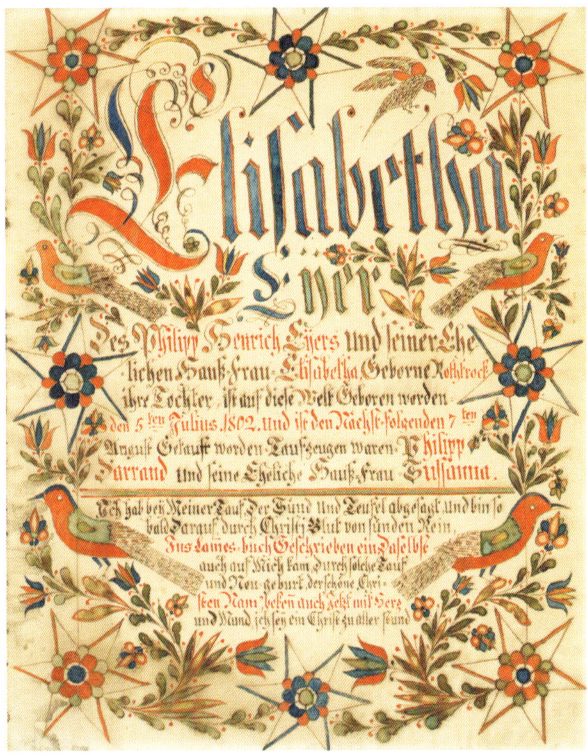
Elisabetha
Eyer
Des Philipp Henrich Eyers und seiner Ehe-
lichen Hauß-Frau Elisabetha Geborne Rothrock
ihre Tochter, ist auf diese Welt Geboren worden
den 5 ten Julius 1802. und ist den Nächst-folgenden 7 ten
August Getauft worden. Taufzeugen waren. Philipp
Farrand und seine Eheliche Hauß-Frau Susanna.

FIG. 12 (LEFT)
Birth and baptismal certificate for Elisabetha Wollfinger. Attributed to Johann Adam Eyer (1755–1837), Hamilton Township, Monroe County, Pennsylvania, c. 1801. Ink and watercolor on laid paper, 10 x 8 in.
FREE LIBRARY OF PHILADELPHIA

FIG. 13 (RIGHT)
Birth and baptismal certificate for Elisabetha Eyer. Attributed to Johann Adam Eyer (1755–1837), Hamilton Township, Monroe County, Pennsylvania, c. 1802. Watercolor and ink on laid paper, 10 x 8 in.
FREE LIBRARY OF PHILADELPHIA

Other types include birth records (used by groups who did not practice infant baptism, such as the Mennonites), rewards of merit, *Vorschriften* (writing samples), *Haus Segen* (house blessings), *Liebesbriefe* (love letters or valentines), New Year's greetings, religious texts, and family records. Also popular were fraktur bookplates used to identify ownership of a cherished Bible, hymnal, or even account book (fig. 11).

Most fraktur artists were schoolmasters, who were literate and had access to the necessary materials: paper, ink, quill pens (metal-point pens were not available until about 1820), and brushes. Pigments were typically acquired in raw, powdered form at an apothecary shop or general store, then mixed with a binder (usually gum arabic) and water. The working process of the artist and visual impact of watercolor decoration can readily be seen by comparing two certificates made by Johann Adam Eyer, a prolific fraktur artist who began teaching school in 1779, for his own nieces (figs. 12, 13). The first, made for Elisabetha Wollfinger, is unfinished. Eyer began by inking the outline of the principal motifs and then wrote the inscription. He used a nearly identical layout on the

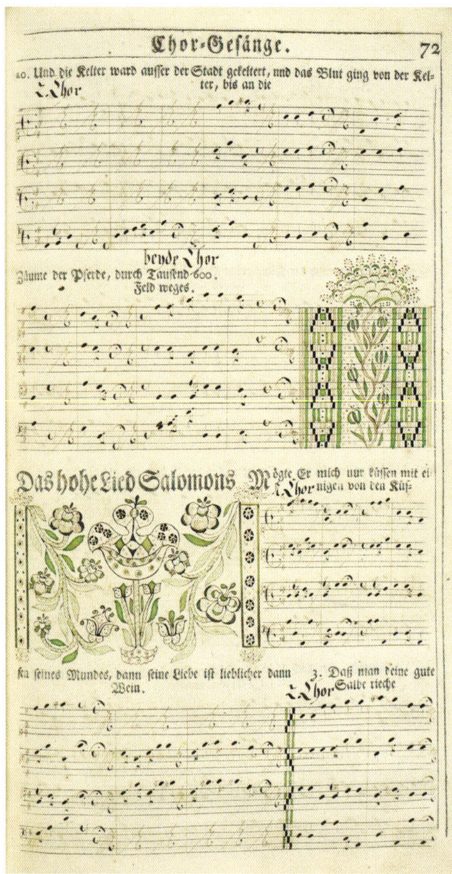

FIG. 14

Paradisisches Wunder-Spiel. Printed and decorated at the Ephrata Cloister, Ephrata, Lancaster County, Pennsylvania, 1754. Watercolor and ink on laid paper, 13⅛ x 8⅝ in. The text on this page is from the Song of Solomon: "Let him kiss me with the kisses of his mouth, for thy love is better than wine."

FREE LIBRARY OF PHILADELPHIA

second certificate, made for Elisabetha Eyer, but the addition of watercolor makes a dramatic difference in its final appearance.

The earliest known reference to the production of fraktur in Pennsylvania dates from 1744, when a visitor to the Ephrata Cloister in Lancaster County observed the inhabitants making decorated manuscripts. Founded about 1732 by Conrad Beissel (1691–1768), Ephrata was a radical Pietist community whose members practiced celibacy, plain dress, limited sleep, fasting, and hard work as the means to spiritual enlightenment. The men farmed the land and ran several mills as well as a printshop, while the women were responsible for textile production and food preparation. Ephrata's inhabitants also made fraktur manuscripts and decorated hymnals such as the *Paradisisches Wunder-Spiel*, first published in 1754 (fig. 14). The words and staves of this edition were printed, while the musical notes and the floral decoration were hand drawn.[2]

BIRTH AND BAPTISMAL CERTIFICATES

The *Geburts-und-Taufschein*, or birth and baptismal certificate, was the most common type of fraktur made in Pennsylvania due to the importance of baptism within the Lutheran and German Reformed faiths. Made in both handwritten and printed formats, these documents typically include extensive genealogical data (child's name, parents' names, location and date of birth and baptism, and godparents' names). The form evolved out of various European precedents, including the *Taufpatenbrief* or *Göttelbrief*, a letter (*Brief*) to the child from the godparents—known as *Taufpaten* in the Palatinate and *Göttel* in the German-speaking region of Alsace in eastern France (fig. 15). The genealogical focus of Pennsylvania certificates is likely due to the chronic shortage of ministers and church recordkeeping in the colony; European versions typically include scant personal data, as there were reliable parish registers to record such information. An unusual hybrid is the baptismal wish, or *Taufwunsch*, made by the anonymous Sussel-Washington Artist (fig. 16). Like its Old World counterparts, the document begins with good wishes and admonitions to the newly baptized child, but it also contains genealogical data more typical of Pennsylvania documents.[3]

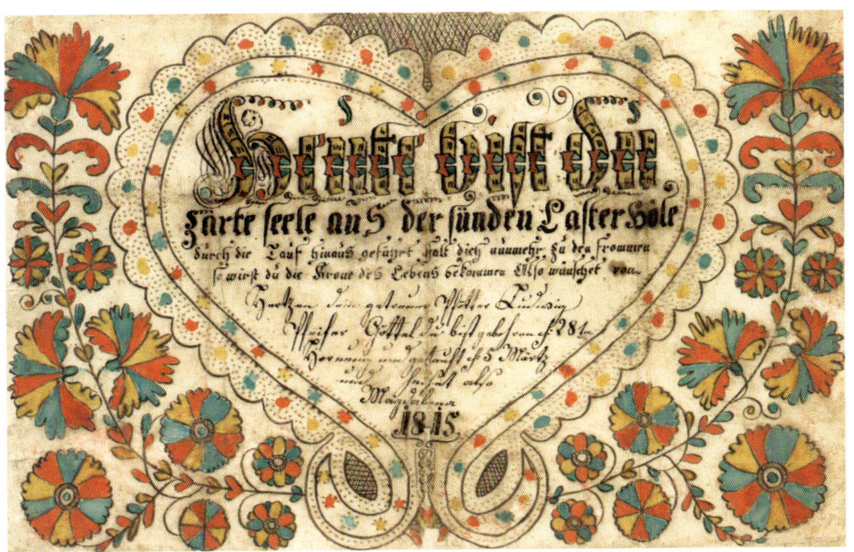

FIG. 15

Letter from the godparents. Alsace, France, 1815. Watercolor and ink on laid paper with pinpricking, 8⅜ x 9½ in. Known as a *Göttelbrief*, this document is inscribed with admonitions from Ludwig Pfeifer to his goddaughter, Magdalena, who was baptized on March 5, 1815.

FREE LIBRARY OF PHILADELPHIA

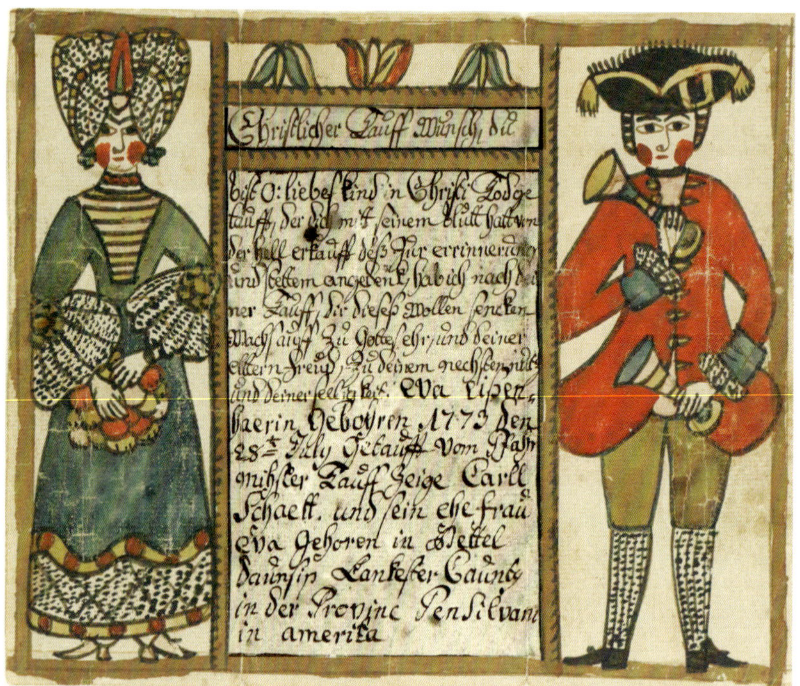

FIG. 16
Baptismal wish for Eva Eissenhaer. Attributed to the Sussel-Washington Artist (active c. 1760–85), Bethel Township, Lancaster (now Lebanon) County, Pennsylvania, c. 1773. Watercolor and ink on laid paper, 6½ x 7⅞ in.
FREE LIBRARY OF PHILADELPHIA

One of the most prolific and influential makers of birth and baptismal certificates was Henrich Otto, who emigrated from Germany in 1753. About 1775, he made an entirely hand-drawn certificate to commemorate the birth and baptism of Maria Elisabeth Müller (fig. 17). Although Otto's decorative motifs—such as leafy vines, tulips, carnations, spiky flowers, and stylized pomegranates—were time-consuming to draw, they exerted tremendous influence on dozens of fraktur artists, including four of his own sons. As demand for birth and baptismal certificates increased, Otto became one of the first artists to use printed versions, which he obtained from the Ephrata printshop by 1784. With pre-printed text and images (made with woodcut stamps), artists filled in the blanks with the customer's genealogical data and applied watercolor, sometimes with additional hand-drawn motifs (fig. 18). By the early 1790s, printed certificates were issued in a triple-heart format. The large central heart contained the genealogical information, flanked by two smaller hearts with verses from a common Lutheran baptismal hymn. Vertically oriented, printed certificates with images of angels were popular from the 1820s to the 1890s. Hand-drawn certificates also continued to be produced well into the 1800s, such as the one made for Susanna Clementine

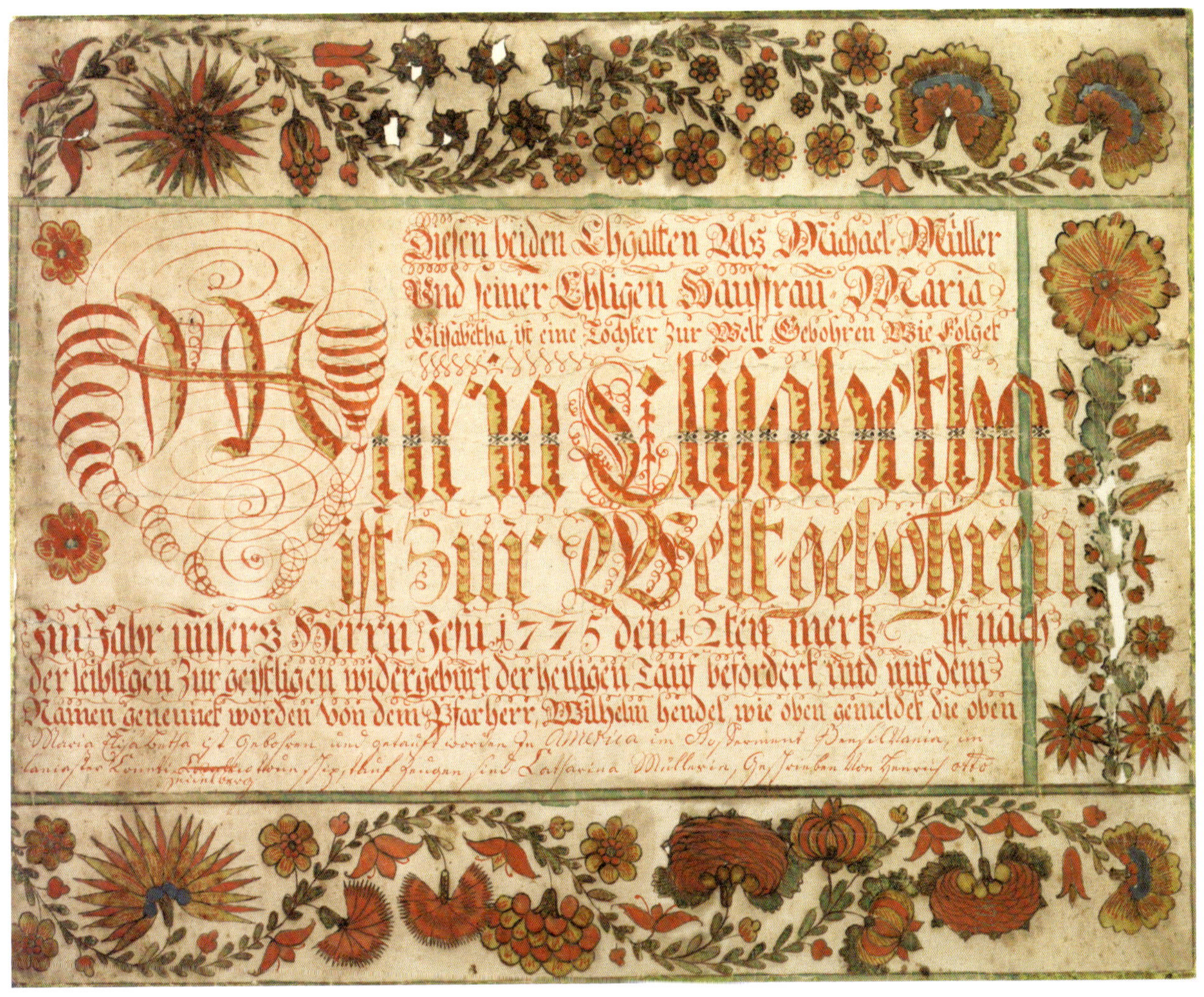

FIG. 17
Birth and baptismal certificate for Maria Elisabeth Müller. Henrich Otto (1733–c. 1799), Millbach area, Lebanon County, Pennsylvania, c. 1775. Watercolor and ink on laid paper, 12¾ x 16⅜ in.
FREE LIBRARY OF PHILADELPHIA

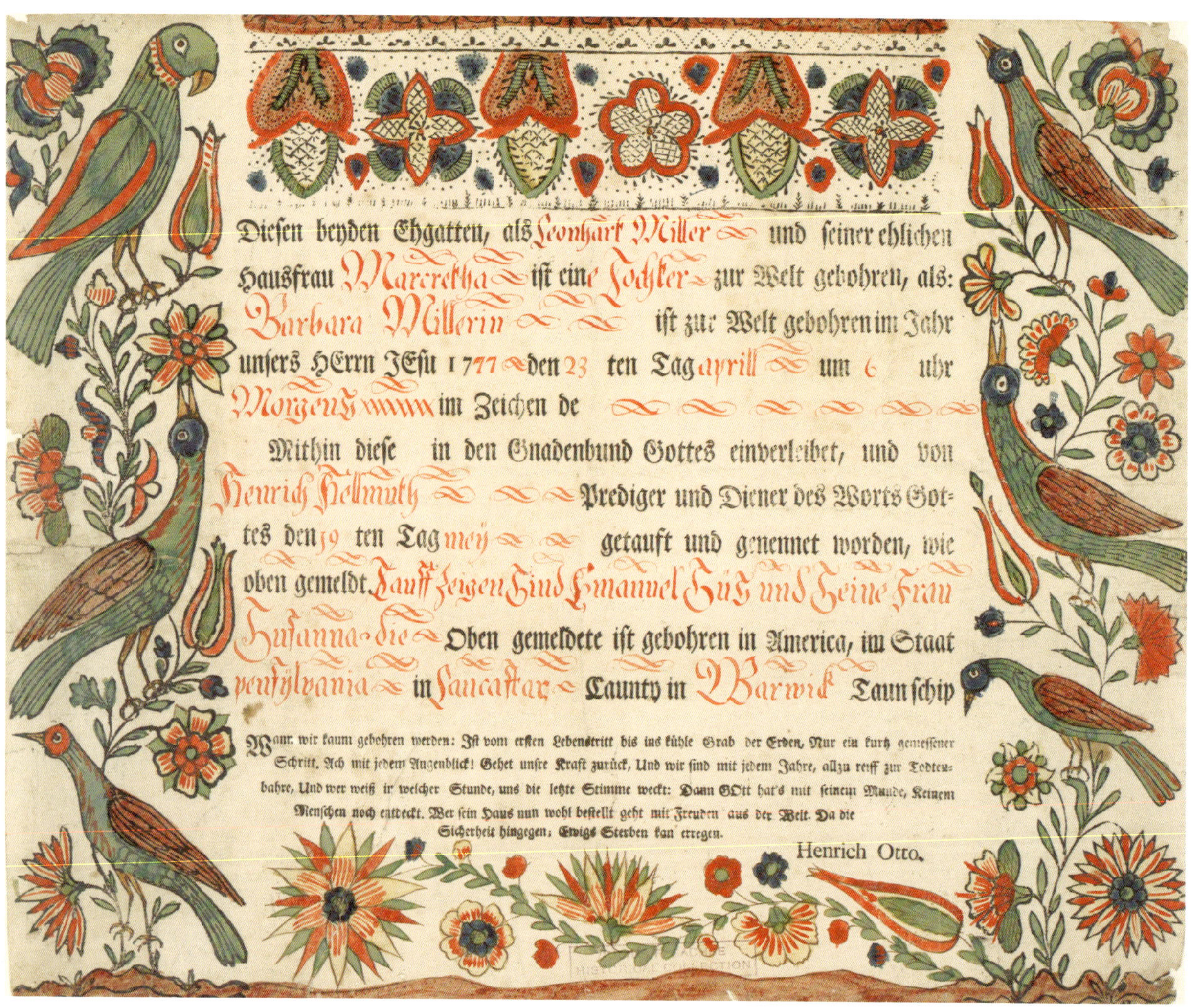

Diesen beyden Ehgatten, als Leonhart Miller und seiner ehlichen Hausfrau Marcretha ist eine Dochter zur Welt gebohren, als: Barbara Millerin ist zur Welt gebohren im Jahr unsers HErrn JEsu 1777 den 23 ten Tag aprill um 6 uhr Morgens im Zeichen de

Mithin diese in den Gnadenbund Gottes einverleibet, und von Henrich Hellmuth Prediger und Diener des Worts Gottes den 19 ten Tag mey getauft und genennet worden, wie oben gemeldt. Tauff Zeigen Sind Emanuel Süs und Seine Frau Susanna die Oben gemeldete ist gebohren in America, im Staat pensylvania in Lancastar Caunty in Warwik Taunschip

Wann wir kaum gebohren werden: Ist vom ersten Lebenstritt bis ins kühle Grab der Erden, Nur ein kurtz gemessener Schritt. Ach mit jedem Augenblick! Gehet unsre Kraft zurück, Und wir sind mit jedem Jahre, allzu reiff zur Todtenbahre, Und wer weiß in welcher Stunde, uns die letzte Stimme weckt: Dann GOtt hat's mit seinem Munde, Keinem Menschen noch entdeckt. Wer sein Haus nun wohl bestellt geht mit Freuden aus der Welt. Da die Sicherheit hingegen; Ewigs Sterben kan erregen.

Henrich Otto.

FIG. 18

Birth and baptismal certificate for Barbara Miller. Decoration after Henrich Otto (1733–c. 1799), printing attributed to the Ephrata Cloister, Ephrata, Lancaster County, Pennsylvania, c. 1785. Watercolor and ink on laid paper, 12¾ x 15¾ in.

FREE LIBRARY OF PHILADELPHIA

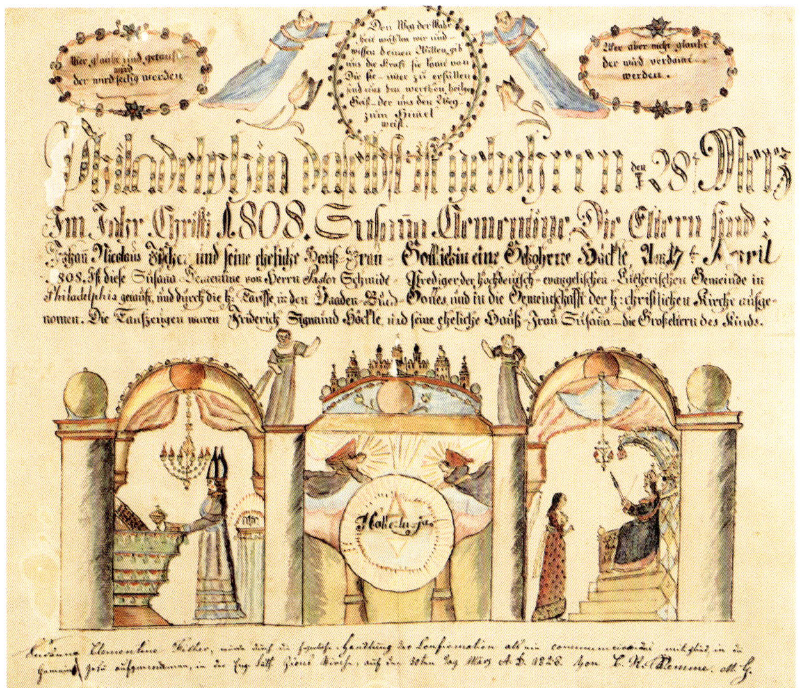

FIG. 19
Birth and baptismal certificate for Susanna Clementine Fisher. Philadelphia, Pennsylvania, c. 1808. Watercolor and ink on laid paper, 12¾ x 15½ in.
FREE LIBRARY OF PHILADELPHIA

Fisher, who was baptized in 1808 at Zion Lutheran Church in Philadelphia (fig. 19). An inscription across the bottom notes that she was confirmed in the same church on March 30, 1828. For reasons that are unclear, fraktur was rarely made in Philadelphia, even though German-speaking people comprised a significant portion of the city's population (as high as 45 percent in 1760) and there were several German-language printers active there throughout the 1700s.[4]

RELIGIOUS DRAWINGS AND TEXTS

Most Pennsylvania Germans were members of the Lutheran or German Reformed faith, including some French Huguenots who had fled to Germany after the revocation of the Edict of Nantes in 1685 and the reemergence of strong Catholic leadership in France. Others were Anabaptists (meaning re-baptized as adults after leaving the church in which they were baptized as infants), including the Amish and Mennonites, who had been persecuted because of their belief in non-resistance and the baptism of adults rather than infants. Religious drawings and texts reflected the diverse faiths of the Pennsylvania Germans, who were free to practice their beliefs in Pennsylvania due to the colony's religious tolerance. Although biblical verses, prayers, and hymns were commonly used as text on fraktur, few artists drew biblical scenes or religious imagery. One of the few who did was Theodore or "Durs" Rudy Sr. or Jr., whose colorful rendering of Christ preaching to his disciples is one of the finest examples of a religious drawing made by a Pennsylvania German fraktur artist (fig. 20). The Rudy family emigrated from Europe in 1803 and by 1809 had settled in Lehigh County, where both Rudy Sr. and Jr. taught school and made fraktur; thus far their work is indistinguishable.[5]

FIG. 20 (RIGHT)
Drawing of Christ preaching to his disciples. Attributed to Durs Rudy Sr. (1766–1843) or Durs Rudy Jr. (1789–1850), Lehigh County, Pennsylvania, 1820–40. Watercolor and ink on wove paper, 8¾ x 6⅝ in.
FREE LIBRARY OF PHILADELPHIA

Most fraktur are not illustrated with such overt religious iconography or symbolism. In Bucks and Montgomery Counties, many of the German-speaking settlers were Mennonite or Schwenkfelder. Samuel Gottschall, a Mennonite, taught school during the 1830s in a schoolhouse built on land owned by his family in Franconia Township, Montgomery County. A religious text he made in 1833 is decorated with flowers and inscribed in the central heart (translation): "Flee from sin, love virtue, make the beginning in youth. Go on and don't give up until you go into your grave" (fig. 21).[6] Conrad Gilbert, who emigrated from Germany in 1750 and became a schoolmaster in Berks County, drew a bouquet of flowers to accompany a quote from Ezekiel 33:11 (translation): "As I live, saith the Lord God, I have no pleasure in the death of the wicked, but that the wicked turn from his ways and live." A religious text made by Susanna Heebner (Hübner), a Schwenkfelder and one of the first female fraktur artists, is embellished with ornate calligraphy and images of birds, tulips, and other flowers (fig. 22). The text begins (translation): "Go forth, my heart, and seek joy in this dear summertime, in God's gifts. Look at the beautiful gardens, and see how they have adorned themselves for me and you." The Schwenkfelders, who hailed primarily from Silesia, immigrated to Pennsylvania in the 1730s and settled in what would later become Montgomery County. Numerous Schwenkfelder ministers, schoolmasters, and young women made fraktur for their family, friends, and students.[7]

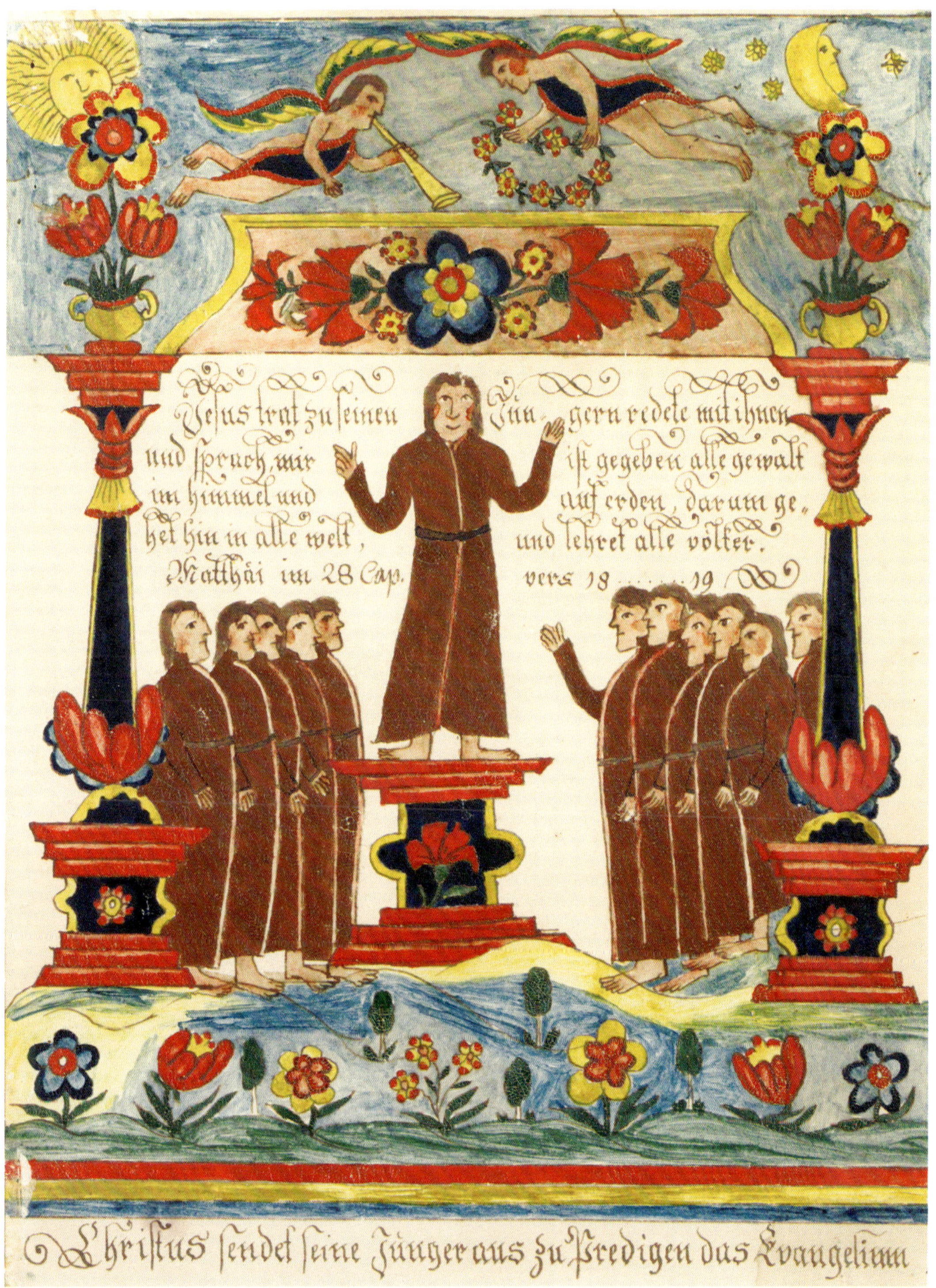
Jesus trat zu seinen Jün gern redete mit ihnen
und sprach, mir ist gegeben alle gewalt
im himmel und auf erden, darum ge,
het hin in alle welt, und lehret alle völker.
Matthäi im 28 Cap. vers 18 19
Christus sendet seine Jünger aus zu Predigen das Evangelium

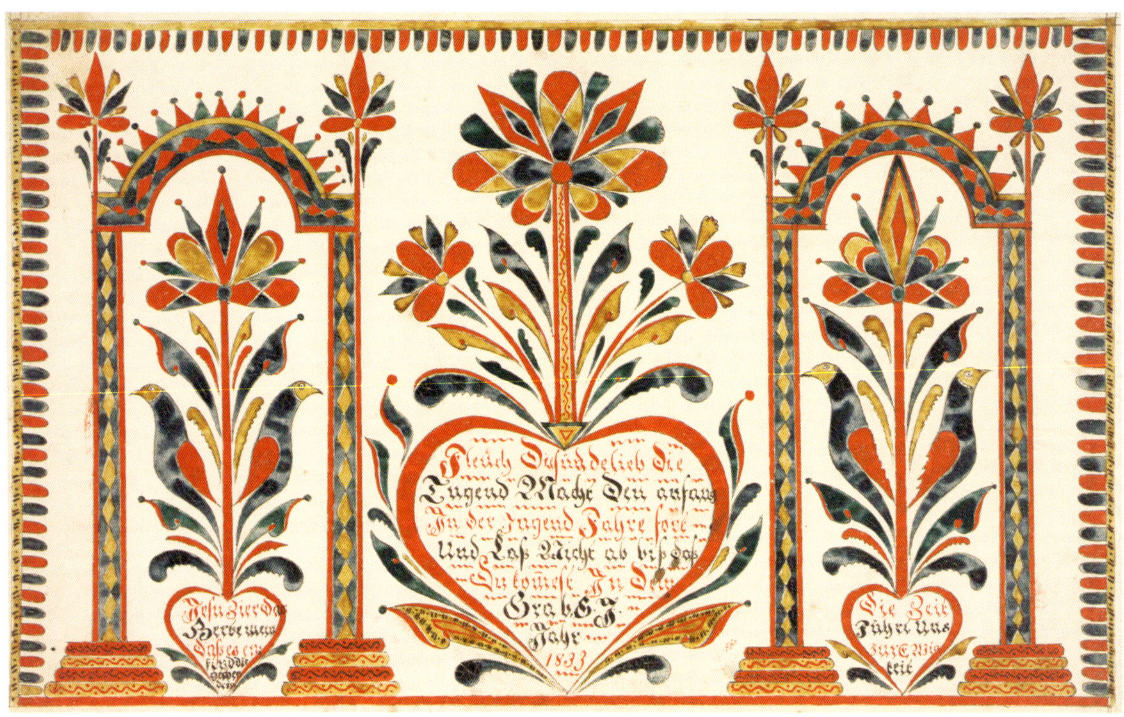
Jahr
1833

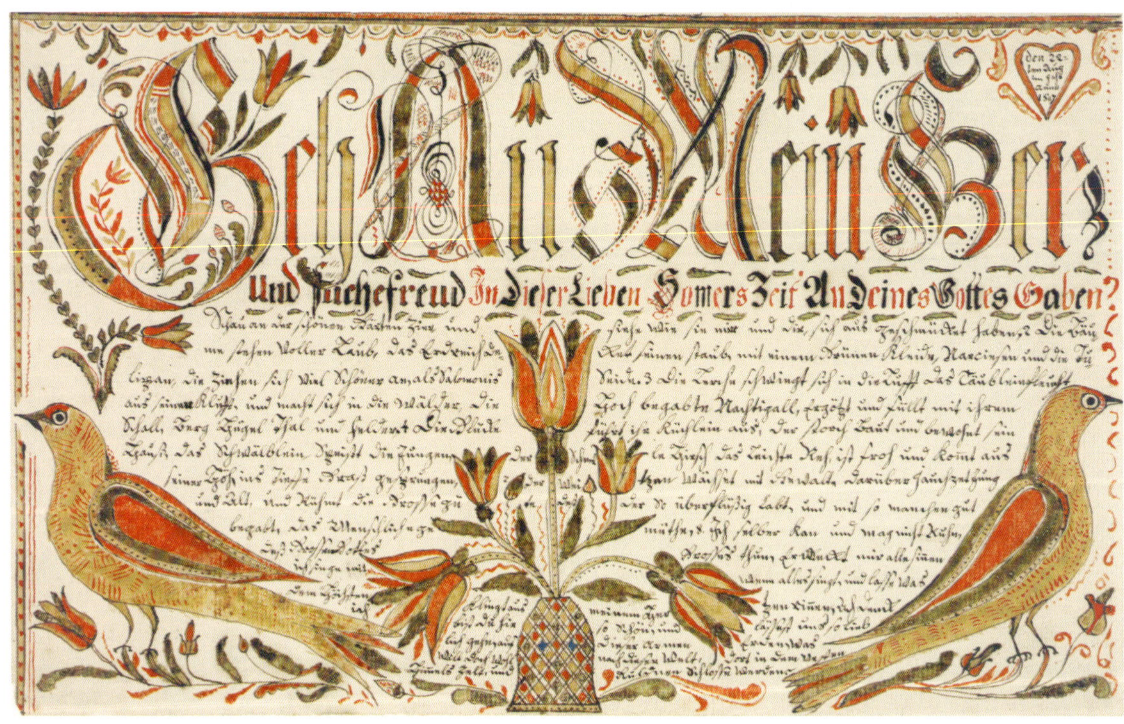
Geh Aus Mein Herz
Und suche Freud In dieser Lieben Somers Zeit An deines Gottes Gaben?

FIG. 21 (LEFT, TOP)
Religious text. Attributed to Samuel Gottschall (1808–1898), Franconia Township, Montgomery County, Pennsylvania, 1833. Watercolor and ink on wove paper, 7¾ x 12⅝ in. Gottschall used a thick binder (probably gum arabic) in his watercolors, resulting in heavily pooled areas of pigment, which are especially notable on this piece in the blue-green foliage.
FREE LIBRARY OF PHILADELPHIA

FIG. 22 (LEFT, BOTTOM)
Religious text. Attributed to Susanna Heebner (1750–1818), Worcester Township, Montgomery County, Pennsylvania, August 22, 1807. Watercolor and ink on laid paper, 8⅛ x 13⅛ in.
FREE LIBRARY OF PHILADELPHIA

EDUCATION

Most Pennsylvania German children were educated in church-affiliated schools prior to the passage in 1834 of the Free Public School Act. School was typically conducted in German, although by the early 1800s students also learned to read and write in English. As many fraktur artists were also schoolmasters, certain types of fraktur developed that were particularly associated with the school system. Christopher Dock, a Mennonite teacher, published a pioneering treatise on educational management in 1770 in which he noted rewarding good students with "a flower drawn on paper or a bird."[8] Most small fraktur drawings of birds, flowers, and other designs were probably made as rewards of merit, although the practice of storing them in books for safekeeping has led many to refer to them as bookmarks (fig. 23). One drawing of flowers with short biblical quote is inscribed on the back for Susanna Scheuer (fig. 24); it was presented to her by Martin Brechall, who taught school in the Berks-Lehigh County border region and was known as a firm disciplinarian. According to one story, Brechall would sit with his back to his students while covertly monitoring them with a mirror to catch troublemakers.[9]

When children were learning to write, schoolmasters often presented them with a special certificate known as a *Vorschrift*, or writing sample. Most begin with a biblical quote or hymn verse and conclude with an alphabet and numeral system. One of the earliest known dated examples of a Pennsylvania German *Vorschrift* was made in 1766 by Hans Jacob Brubacher, a Mennonite farmer and schoolmaster in Lancaster County (fig. 25). It begins with a verse from Matthew 20:1–16 (the parable of the workers in the vineyard) and concludes with the inscription (translation): "This writing sample belongs to me, David Herr." Almost forty years later, schoolmaster Christian Alsdorff of Earl Township, Lancaster County, used the same basic format to make a writing sample for his pupil Anna Scherg (fig. 26). For the text, he selected a fitting passage from Proverbs 4:13 (translation): "Take hold of instruction and do not let it go, for it is your life."[10]

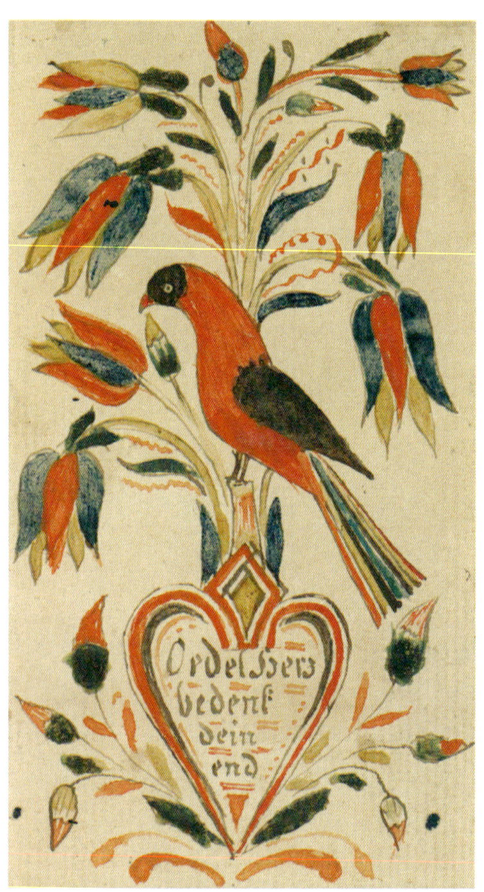

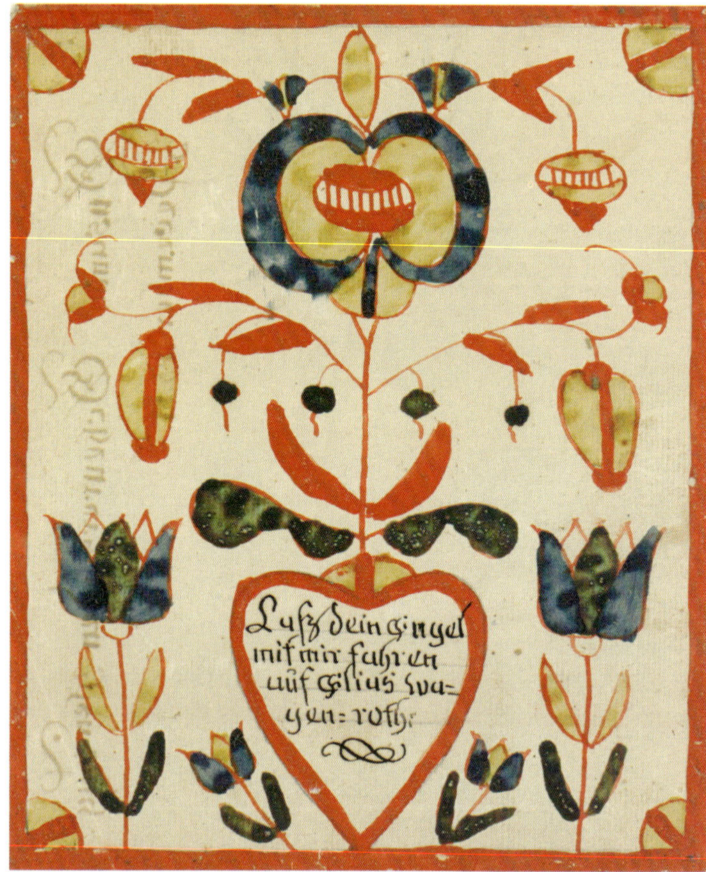

FIG. 23

Reward of merit (drawing of a bird and flowers). School of Andreas Kolb (1749–1811), Montgomery County, Pennsylvania, c. 1800. Watercolor and ink on laid paper, 5 x 2¾ in. Inscribed within the heart at the bottom is the text (translation): "O noble heart, bethink your end," a common phrase in Mennonite fraktur and needlework reminding one to prepare for death.

FREE LIBRARY OF PHILADELPHIA

FIG. 24

Reward of merit for Susanna Scheuer. Attributed to Martin Brechall (c. 1757–1831), Lehigh County, Pennsylvania, December 3, 1811. Watercolor and ink on laid paper, 7¾ x 6½ in. This fraktur is inscribed (translation): "Let your angels ride with me in Elias's chariot of fire," a reference to Elijah's entrance to heaven in 2 Kings 2:11.

FREE LIBRARY OF PHILADELPHIA

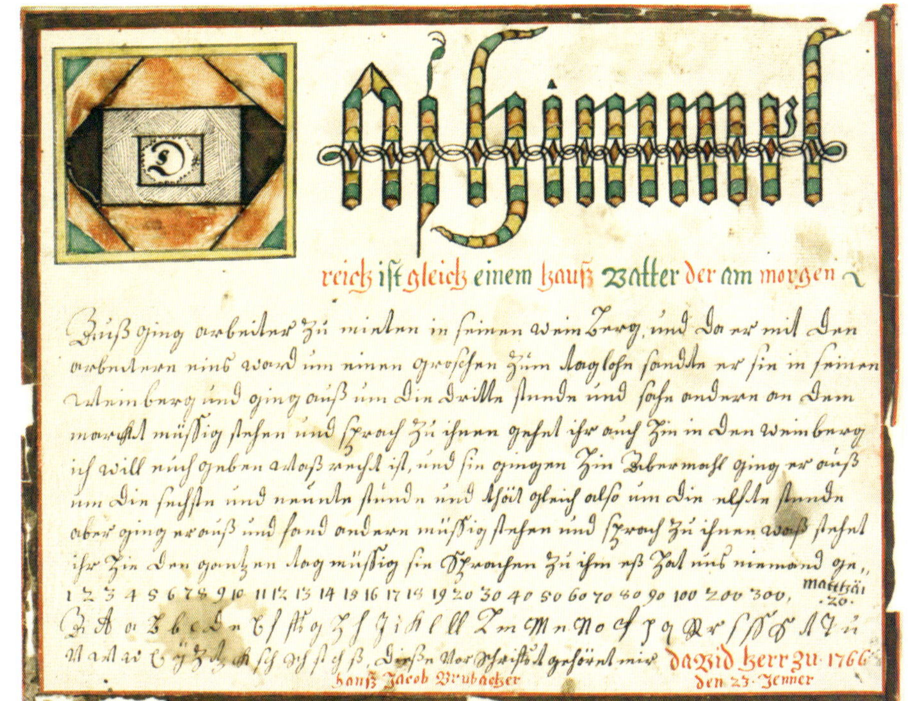

FIG. 25 (RIGHT)
Writing sample for David Herr. Hans Jacob Brubacher (c. 1730–1802), Providence Township, Lancaster County, Pennsylvania, January 23, 1766. Watercolor and ink on laid paper, 7⅛ x 9⅛ in.
FREE LIBRARY OF PHILADELPHIA

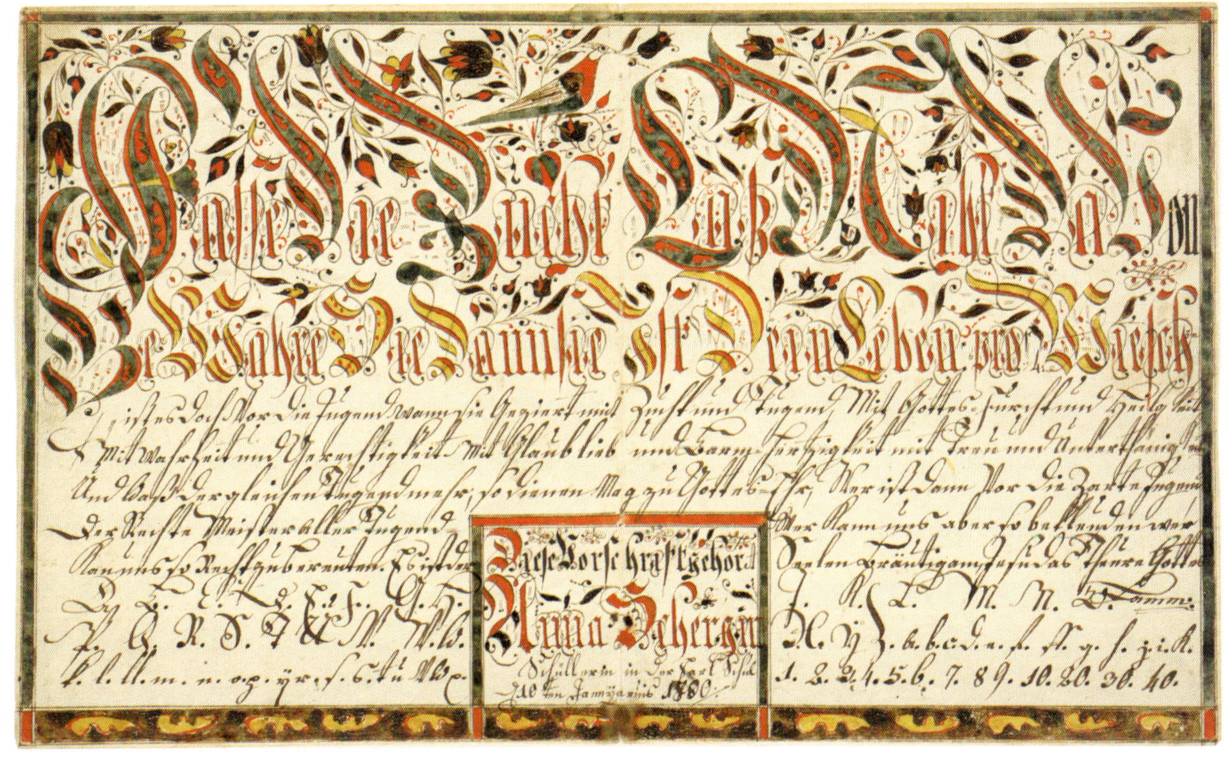

FIG. 26 (BELOW)
Writing sample for Anna Scherg. Attributed to Christian Alsdorff (c. 1760–1838), Earl Township, Lancaster County, Pennsylvania, January 10, 1800. Watercolor and ink on laid paper, 7¾ x 13 in.
FREE LIBRARY OF PHILADELPHIA

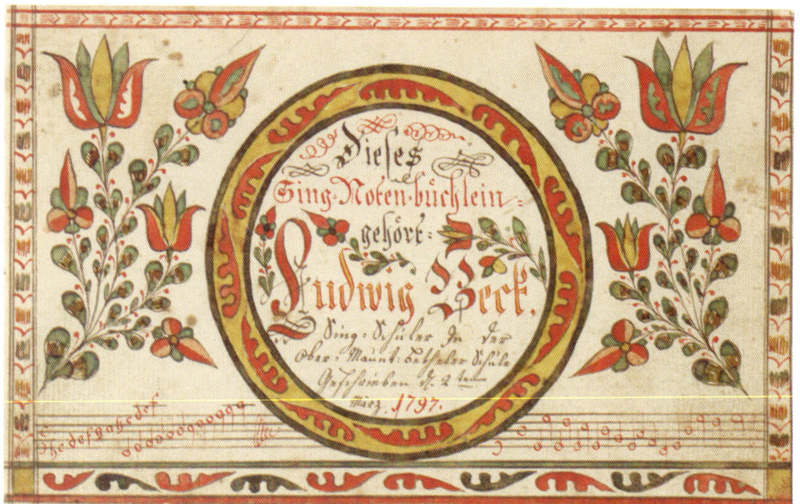

FIG. 27
Tune book with bookplate for Ludwig Beck. Attributed to Johann Adam Eyer (1755–1837). Upper Mount Bethel School, Northampton County, Pennsylvania, March 2, 1797. Watercolor and ink on laid paper, 4 x 6½ in.
FREE LIBRARY OF PHILADELPHIA

Many schoolmasters also provided instruction in vocal music; some even made decorated bookplates for their students' tune books and hymnals. About 1792, Johann Adam Eyer moved from Bucks County to Upper Mount Bethel Township, Northampton County, where he made a bookplate for Ludwig Beck, "singing student," in 1797 (fig. 27). Decorated with flowers and a geometric border, the bookplate features a musical staff along the bottom. A schoolmaster for nearly forty years, Eyer influenced the work of many other fraktur artists. Foremost among them was David Kulp (or Kolb), whom Eyer taught from 1782 to 1786. In 1783, when Kulp was just six years old, Eyer presented him with a bookplate for his hymnal (fig. 28). Kulp began teaching at the Deep Run School in 1801. Like Eyer, he was also a fraktur artist and made tune books and decorated bookplates for many of his pupils. At the end of the spring term in 1803, Kulp presented Anna Landes with a bookplate for her catechism (fig. 29). Protected inside the book's cover for more than two hundred years, it retains much of its original vibrancy.[11]

BEYOND SOUTHEASTERN PENNSYLVANIA

Southeastern Pennsylvania was by no means the only region in which fraktur was produced. By the mid-to-late 1700s, some Pennsylvania Germans began to move beyond the region's borders in search of more land and better economic opportunities. Many traveled southward into the Shenandoah Valley of Virginia, while others headed to western

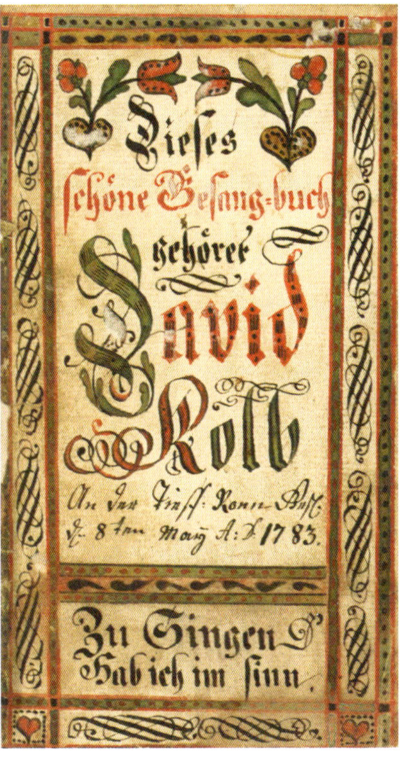

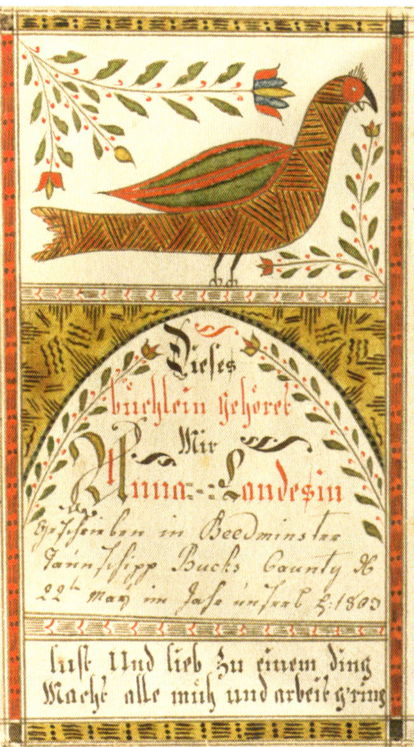

FIG. 28 (LEFT)
Hymnal with bookplate for David Kolb. Attributed to Johann Adam Eyer (1755–1837), Deep Run School, Bedminster Township, Bucks County, Pennsylvania, May 8, 1783. Watercolor and ink on laid paper, 5¾ x 3¼ in. This fraktur is inscribed (translation): “This beautiful song book belongs to David Kolb on the Deep Run. Written the 8th of May A.D. 1783. To sing is on my mind.”
FREE LIBRARY OF PHILADELPHIA

FIG. 29 (RIGHT)
Catechism with bookplate for Anna Landes. Attributed to David Kulp (1777–1834), Bedminster Township, Bucks County, Pennsylvania, May 22, 1803. Watercolor and ink on laid paper, 5¼ x 3⅛ in.
FREE LIBRARY OF PHILADELPHIA

Pennsylvania or Ohio. Beginning in 1786, dozens of Mennonite families moved north to the Niagara Peninsula in Ontario, Canada. A birth certificate made for Johanna Flori (Flory) evinces this outward migration (fig. 30). Born on March 21, 1800, in Elk Lick Township, Somerset County, Pennsylvania, Johanna was the great-granddaughter of German émigré Joseph Flory, who arrived in Philadelphia in 1733. Her family moved in 1806 to southwestern Ohio, where they settled in Madison Township, Montgomery County—part of the Miami River Valley—and joined the Wolf Creek Dunker or Dunkard Church. There, in 1815, Johanna received a birth certificate made by schoolmaster David Cordier. Little is known of Cordier himself, but many of the families for whom he made certificates were recent arrivals in the Miami River Valley from other regions and even states.[12]

Wherever the Pennsylvania Germans settled, they took with them the tradition of making fraktur and, in many cases, actual documents. The fraktur tradition flourished into the mid-1800s and beyond, with printed birth and baptismal certificates continuing to dominate. Some

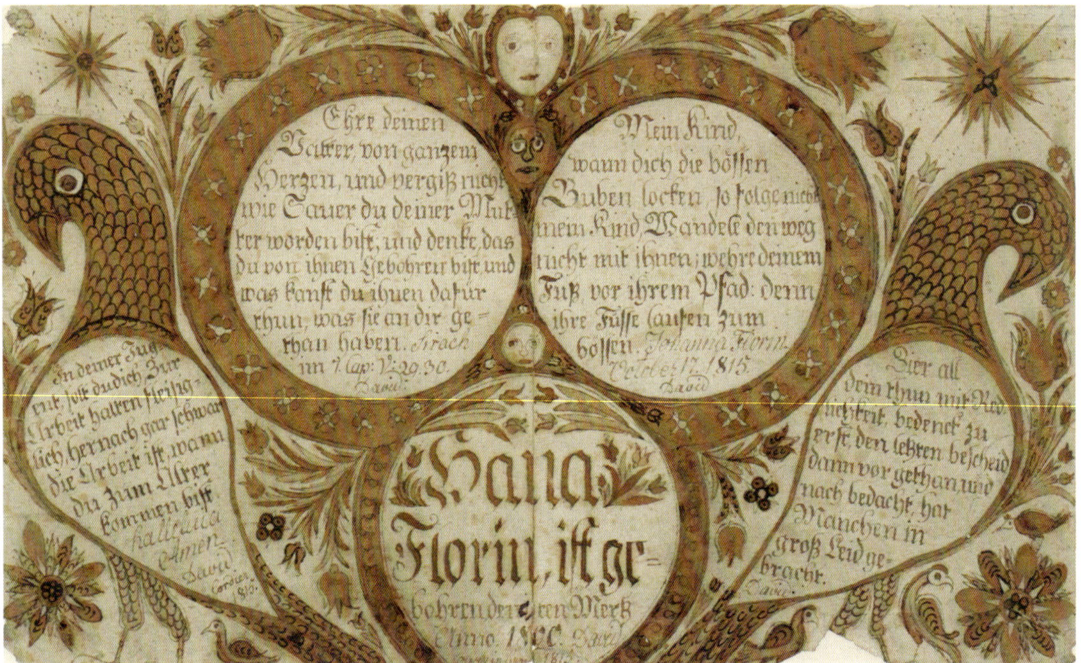

artists did, however, continue to make hand-drawn fraktur, such as Barbara Ebersol, an Amish woman who made fraktur bookplates and drawings until her death in 1922. By the early 1900s, rising antiquarian interest in fraktur was spurred by the colonial revival movement and the publication of studies such as Henry Chapman Mercer's 1897 essay "The Survival of the Medieval Art of Illuminative Writing among Pennsylvania Germans."[13]

FIG. 30
Birth certificate for Johanna Flori. David Cordier (active c. 1805–20), Montgomery County, Ohio, October 17, 1815. Ink on laid paper, 7¾ x 12¾ in.
FREE LIBRARY OF PHILADELPHIA

In Montgomery County, Pennsylvania, John Derstine Souder (1865–1942) spent the last five years of his life making copies of original fraktur documents in what he described as a "modern revival of manuscripts embellished part pen work." His reproductions are now treasured as a unique form of fraktur revivalism (fig. 31).[14] Modern artists such as Elie Nadelman collected fraktur and took inspiration from it and other types of Pennsylvania German folk art, while dozens of other artists continue to make fraktur today, both as works of art and as commemorative documents made on commission. Even as genealogical information is more accessible than ever and the need to record such data via handmade certificates no longer necessary, there remains a deeply rooted appreciation for fraktur. Contemporary artists such as those featured in this catalogue

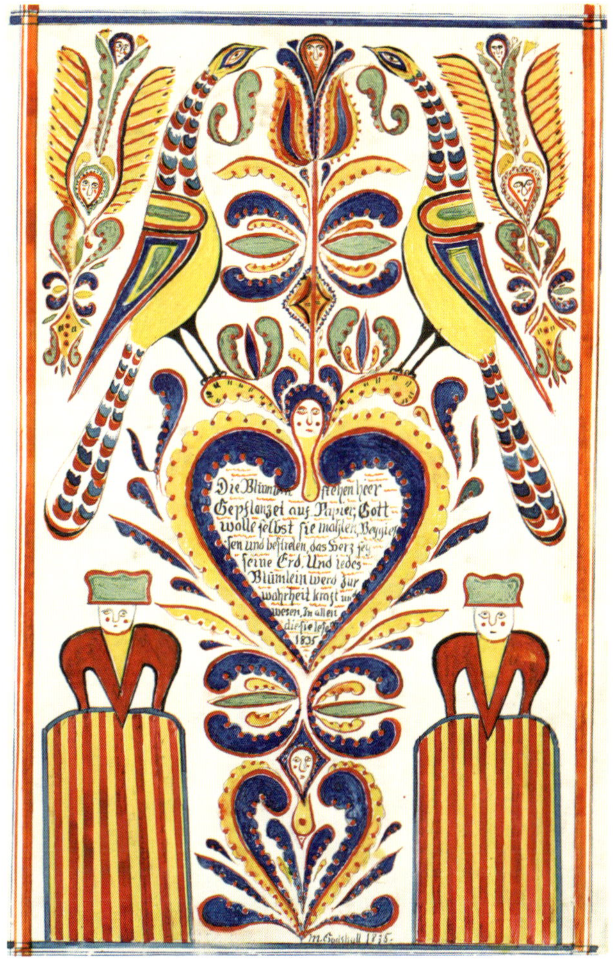

FIG. 31

Religious text. John Derstine Souder (1865–1942), Telford, Montgomery County, Pennsylvania, 1939. Watercolor and ink on wove paper, 13 x 9½ in. This colorful fraktur by Souder — an elderly widower and retired storekeeper, postmaster, and farmer — was based on an earlier example, dated 1835 and attributed to Mennonite schoolmaster Samuel Gottschall (see fig. 21 for an example of Gottschall's work).

FREE LIBRARY OF PHILADELPHIA

also incorporate words and images in their own work in ways that evoke the fraktur tradition. No doubt fraktur has changed greatly since it arrived along with the first German-speaking settlers who began immigrating to Pennsylvania in 1683, but it has never disappeared.

NOTES

1 On German immigration to Pennsylvania, see Marianne S. Wokeck, *Trade in Strangers: The Beginnings of Mass Migration to North America* (University Park: Pennsylvania State University Press, 1999), esp. 37–46, 53. On the Pennsylvania Germans' religious diversity, see Donald F. Durnbaugh, "Pennsylvania's Crazy Quilt of German Religious Groups," *Pennsylvania History* 68, no. 1 (Winter 2001): 8–30. On Pennsylvania's population in 1790, see James T. Lemon, *The Best Poor Man's*

Country: A Geographical Study of Early Southeastern Pennsylvania (Baltimore: Johns Hopkins University Press, 1972), 14, 18. On Philadelphia's population in 1800, see tables 1 and 2 in Robert J. Gough, "The Philadelphia Economic Elite at the End of the Eighteenth Century," in *Shaping a National Culture: The Philadelphia Experience, 1750–1800*, ed. Catherine E. Hutchins (Winterthur, DE: Henry Francis du Pont Winterthur Museum, 1994), 18–19.

2 On Ephrata, see Jeffrey Bach, *Voices of the Turtledoves: The Sacred World of Ephrata*, Publications of the Pennsylvania German Society, vol. 36 (University Park: Pennsylvania State University Press, 2006).

3 On European precedents, see Don Yoder, "The European Background of Pennsylvania's Fraktur Art," in *Bucks County Fraktur*, ed. Cory M. Amsler, Publications of the Pennsylvania German Society, vol. 33 (Kutztown, PA: Pennsylvania German Society and the Bucks County Historical Society, 1999), 15–41. On the evolution of the baptismal certificate in Pennsylvania, see Russell D. Earnest and Corinne P. Earnest, *The Heart of the Taufschein: Fraktur and the Pivotal Role of Berks County, Pennsylvania*, Publications of the Pennsylvania German Society, vol. 46 (Kutztown, PA: Pennsylvania German Society, 2012), esp. 7–32, 219–23.

4 On Otto, see Lisa Minardi, "From Millbach to Mahantongo: Fraktur and Furniture of the Pennsylvania Germans," in *American Furniture*, ed. Luke Beckerdite (Hanover, NH: University Press of New England for the Chipstone Foundation, 2011), 60–75. On Philadelphia's German population in 1760, see Marie Basile McDaniel, "Processes of Identity Formation among German Speakers, 1730–1760," in *A Peculiar Mixture: German-Language Cultures and Identities in Eighteenth-Century North America*, ed. Oliver Scheiding and Jan Stievermann (University Park: Pennsylvania State University Press, 2013), 189.

5 Durnbaugh, "Pennsylvania's Crazy Quilt of German Religious Groups," 8–30. On Rudy, see Minardi, *Drawn with Spirit: Pennsylvania German Fraktur from the Joan and Victor Johnson Collection* (Philadelphia: Philadelphia Museum of Art, 2015), 129–34, 305–6.

6 On Gottschall, see Minardi, *Drawn with Spirit*, 116–7, 301; Mary Jane Lederach Hershey, *This Teaching I Present: Fraktur from the Skippack and Lower Salford Mennonite Meetinghouse Schools, 1747–1836* (Intercourse, PA: Good Books, 2003), 171.

7 On Schwenkfelder fraktur, see Minardi, *Drawn with Spirit*, 119–27, 302–4; Dennis K. Moyer, *Fraktur Writings and Folk Art Drawings of the Schwenkfelder Library Collection*, Publications of the Pennsylvania German Society, vol. 31 (Kutztown, PA: Pennsylvania German Society, 1997).

8 Hershey, *This Teaching I Present*, 31.

9 On Brechall, see Minardi, *Drawn with Spirit*, 144–5, 308–9; Russell D. Earnest and Corinne P. Earnest, *Papers for Birth Dayes: A Guide to the Fraktur Artists and Scriveners*, rev. ed. (East Berlin, PA: R. D. Earnest Associates, 1997), vol. 1, 117.

10 On Brubacher, see Minardi, *Drawn with Spirit*, 170–1, 316–7; David R. Johnson, "Hans Jacob Brubacher, Fraktur Artist," *Pennsylvania Mennonite Heritage* 9, no. 1 (January 1986), 11–17. On Alsdorff, see Minardi, *Drawn with Spirit*, 96–99, 294–5; David R. Johnson, "Christian Alsdorff, the Earl Township Artist," *Der Reggeboge: Journal of the Pennsylvania German Society* 20, no. 2 (1980): 45–59.

11 On Eyer, see Minardi, *Drawn with Spirit*, 74–80, 288–9; Frederick S. Weiser, "IAE SD: The Story of Johann Adam Eyer, Schoolmaster and Fraktur Artist, with a Translation of His Roster Book, 1779–1787," in *Ebbes fer Alle-Ebber, Ebbes fer Dich: Something for Everyone—Something for You*, ed. Frederick S. Weiser, Publications of the Pennsylvania German Society, vol. 14 (Breinigsville, PA: Pennsylvania German Society, 1980), 449–60. On Kulp, see Minardi, *Drawn with Spirit*, 86–87, 291; Joel D. Alderfer, "David Kulp, His Hand and Pen, Beet It if You Can: The Bucks County Brown Leaf Artist Identified," in *Bucks County Fraktur*, ed. Cory M. Amsler, Publications of the Pennsylvania German Society, vol. 33 (Kutztown, PA: Pennsylvania German Society and the Bucks County Historical Society, 1999), 151–65.

12 On Cordier, see Minardi, *Drawn with Spirit*, 221, 330–1.

13 On Ebersol, see David Luthy, *Amish Folk Artist Barbara Ebersol: Her Life, Fraktur, and Death Record Book* (Lancaster, PA: Lancaster Mennonite Historical Society, 1995); Henry Chapman Mercer, "The Survival of the Medieval Art of Illuminative Writing among Pennsylvania Germans," in *Proceedings of the American Philosophical Society* 36, no. 156 (September 1897), 424–33.

14 On Souder, see John L. Ruth, "My Work is Symbolical: John D. Souder's Fraktur, 1937–1942," in *Der Reggeboge: Journal of the Pennsylvania German Society* 46, no. 2 (2012): 37–65; quotation on p. 52.

Lisa Minardi is an assistant curator at Winterthur Museum and a doctoral candidate in the History of American Civilization at the University of Delaware. A specialist in Pennsylvania German art, Minardi is the author of Drawn with Spirit: Pennsylvania German Fraktur from the Joan and Victor Johnson Collection *(Philadelphia Museum of Art, 2015) and* A Colorful Folk: Pennsylvania Germans and the Art of Everyday Life *(Winterthur, 2015).*

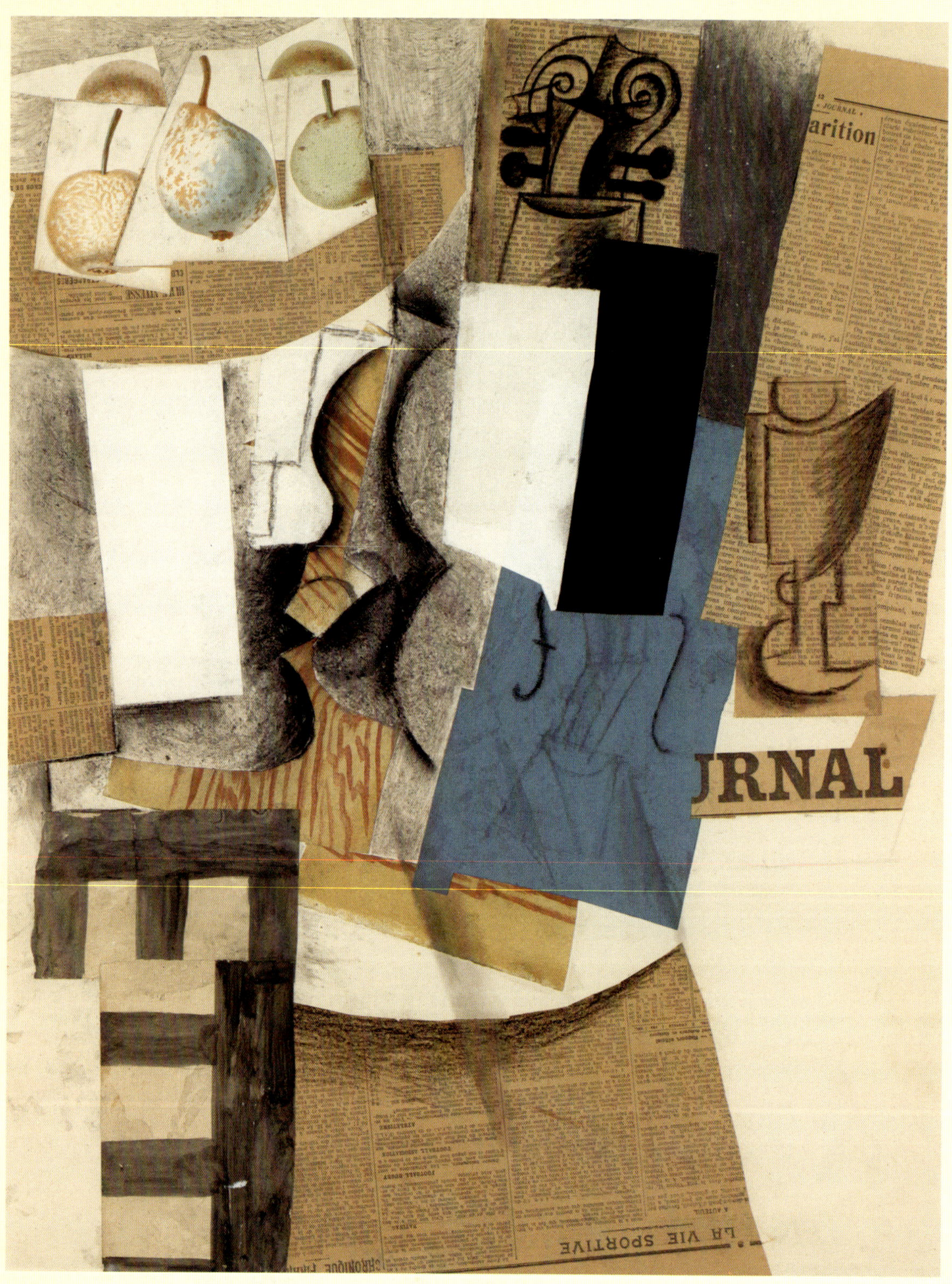
arition
URNAL
LA VIE SPORTIVE

MATTHEW F. SINGER

IN OTHER WORDS: THE SPIRIT OF FRAKTUR IN MODERN AND CONTEMPORARY ART

FIG. 32
Pablo Picasso, *Bowl with Fruit, Violin, and Wineglass*, 1913. Charcoal, chalk, watercolor, oil paint, and coarse charcoal or pigment in binding medium on applied papers, mounted on cardboard, 25½ x 19½ in.
PHILADELPHIA MUSEUM OF ART: A. E. GALLATIN COLLECTION, 1952. © 2015 ESTATE OF PABLO PICASSO / ARTISTS RIGHTS SOCIETY (ARS), NEW YORK

Countless artists have paired words and image, but fraktur did far more than that: flawlessly beautiful or quirky, it commemorated people and events and/or expressed identity, whether personal, group, or communal. Looking at the evolution of modern and contemporary art with fraktur-inspired matters of image and text, commemoration, and identity in mind reveals unexpected but revelatory parallels between otherwise wildly disparate forms of art. Even Cubism and Dada—the early-modern movements that broke most radically with the past—carried an echo of fraktur in their celebration of a particular time and place within a community. Picasso's *Bowl with Fruit, Violin, and Wineglass* (1913; fig. 32) presents recurring Cubist motifs, everyday objects that evoke hours spent in Parisian cafés and boîtes, and bits of text on newspaper that immortalize a moment. The Dadaists—well known for incorporating nonsense text in their visual art, published pieces, and performances—captured the disparity between European ideals and the build-up to World War I, with art as absurd as Europe's circumstances. The life-recording and -affirming spirit of fraktur can be found in work by Marcel Duchamp (1887–1968), whose Dadaist art is noted for its cerebralism and lack of sentiment. His *Apolinère Enameled* (1916–17; fig. 33), an homage to his friend the poet and writer Guillaume Apollinaire (1880–1918), began as a printed-tin advertisement for Sapolin enamel. Here Duchamp blurred the line between utilitarian, commemorative, and artistic painting.

While European modernists looked to African and Oceanic art for ingenious examples of abstracted representation, American modernists such as Elie Nadelman, Marguerite and William Zorach, and Charles Sheeler found it in the nation's folk art. They gathered in salons at the

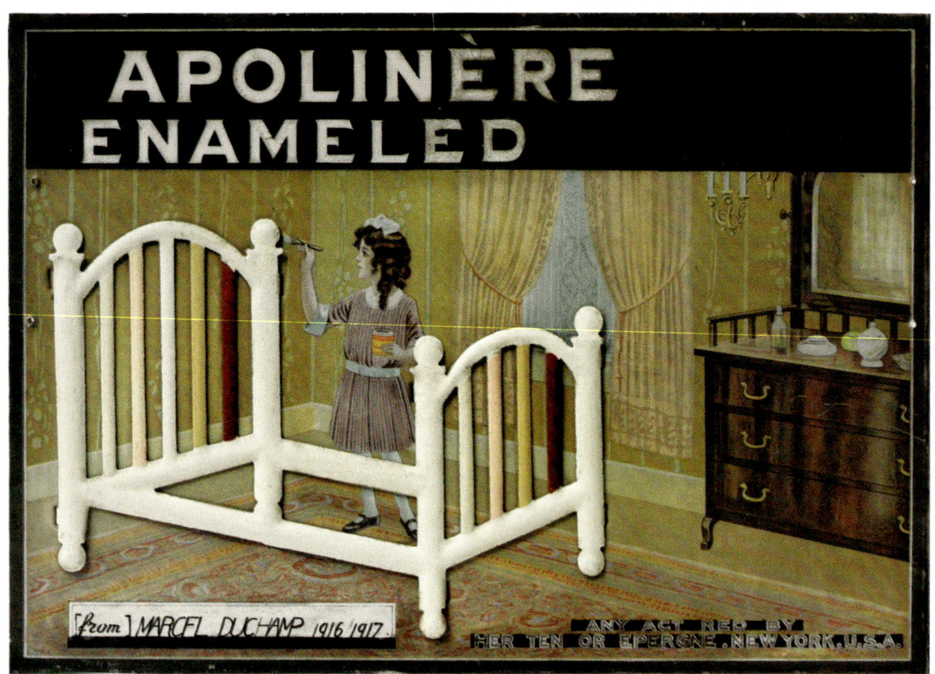

FIG. 33

Marcel Duchamp, *Apolinère Enameled*, 1916–17. Gouache and graphite on painted tin, mounted on cardboard, 9⅝ x 13⅜ in.

PHILADELPHIA MUSEUM OF ART: THE LOUISE AND WALTER ARENSBERG COLLECTION, 1950.

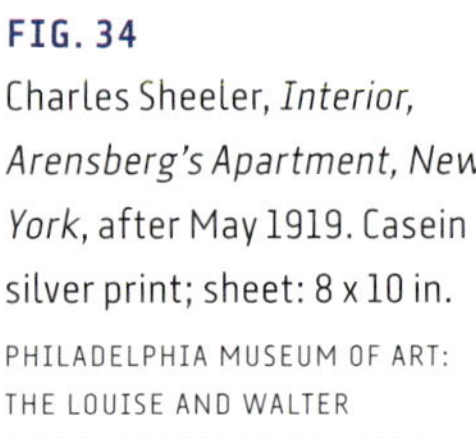

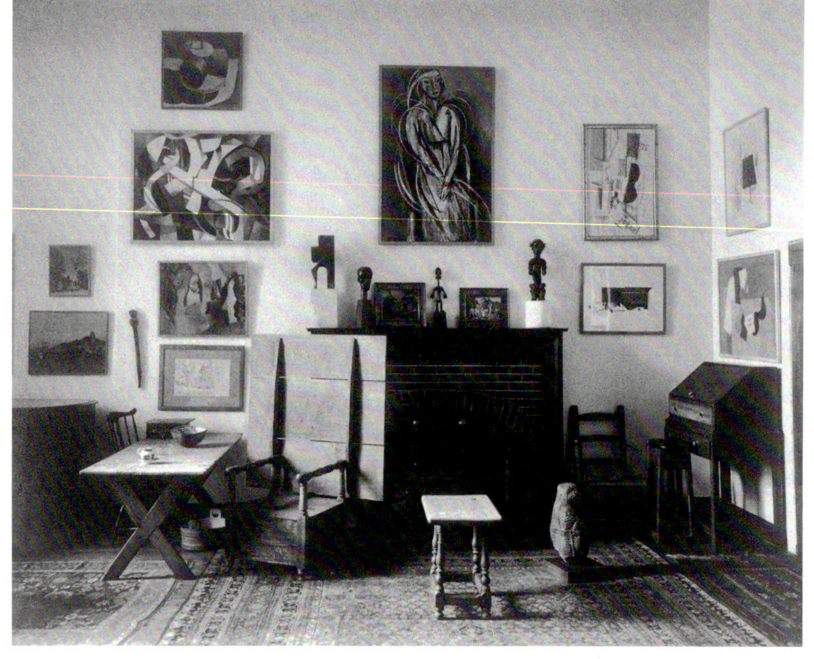

FIG. 34

Charles Sheeler, *Interior, Arensberg's Apartment, New York*, after May 1919. Casein silver print; sheet: 8 x 10 in.

PHILADELPHIA MUSEUM OF ART: THE LOUISE AND WALTER ARENSBERG COLLECTION, 1950

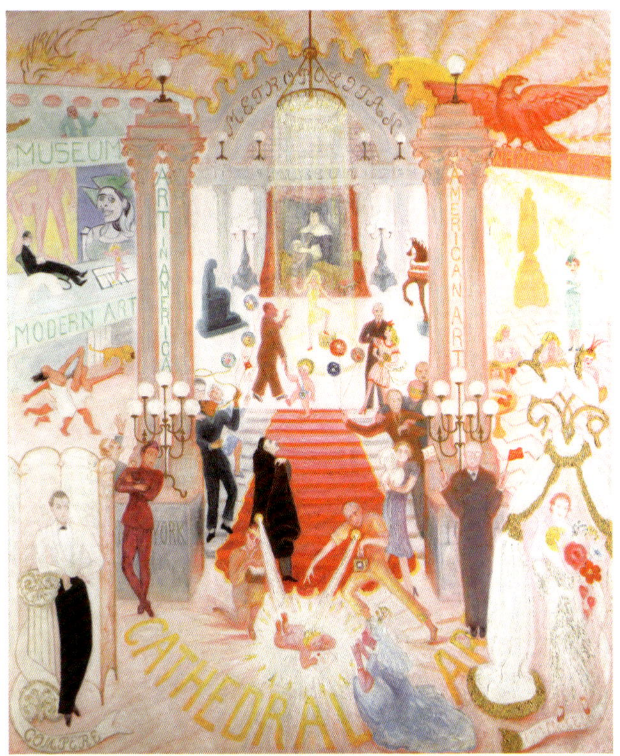

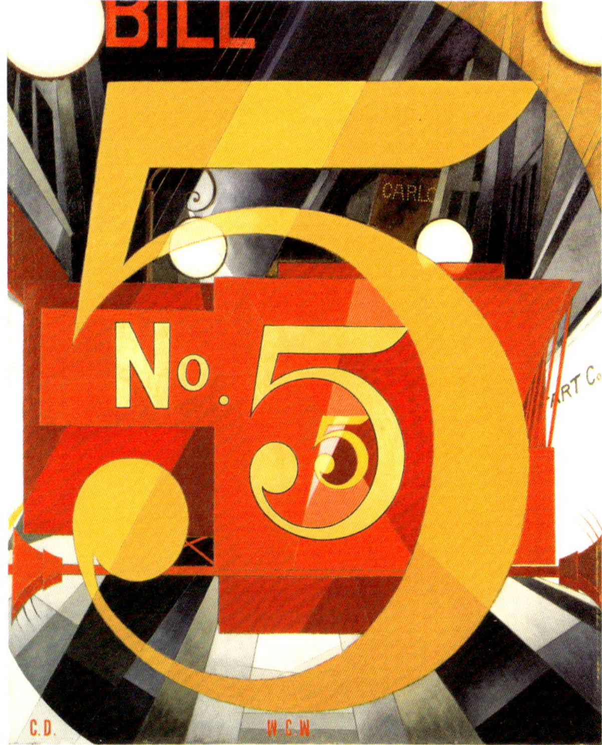

FIG. 35 (LEFT)
Florine Stettheimer, *The Cathedrals of Art*, 1942.
Oil on canvas, 60¼ x 50¼ in.
METROPOLITAN MUSEUM OF ART: GIFT OF ETTIE STETTHEIMER, 1953. © 2015 ARTISTS RIGHTS SOCIETY (ARS), NEW YORK

FIG. 36 (RIGHT)
Charles Demuth, *I Saw the Figure 5 in Gold*, 1928. Oil, graphite, ink, and gold leaf on paperboard (Upson board), 35½ x 30 in.
METROPOLITAN MUSEUM OF ART: ALFRED STIEGLITZ COLLECTION, 1949. © ARTISTS RIGHTS SOCIETY (ARS), NEW YORK

home of pioneering collectors Louise and Walter Arensberg, where masterpieces by Constantin Brancusi, Duchamp, Matisse, and other European and American artists were paired with Shaker and other American folk furniture (fig. 34). Florine Stettheimer (1871–1944) made works that themselves resemble folk art, including her series of large-scale depictions of the secular "cathedrals" of modern New York—such as museums—and their supplicants (fig. 35). Charles Demuth (1883–1935) was a native of Lancaster, Pennsylvania, where his family first settled in 1770, but he traveled often to New York and Europe. He made a series of "poster portraits" of his friends and fellow artists, including *I Saw the Figure Five in Gold (Homage to William Carlos Williams)* (1928; fig. 36).

Commemorative portraits such as Demuth's both expressed and asserted community, thereby becoming statements of identity. This approach became more common in the latter half of the century, as art became increasingly political. Andy Warhol (1928–1987), for example, drew the feet of a hero of his, English photographer Cecil Beaton, giving shape to the then-novel idea of a gay cultural lineage (fig. 37). Women

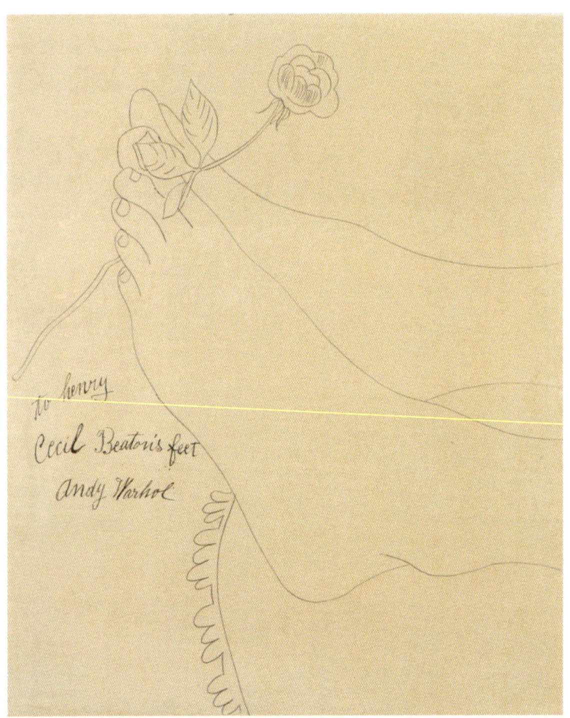

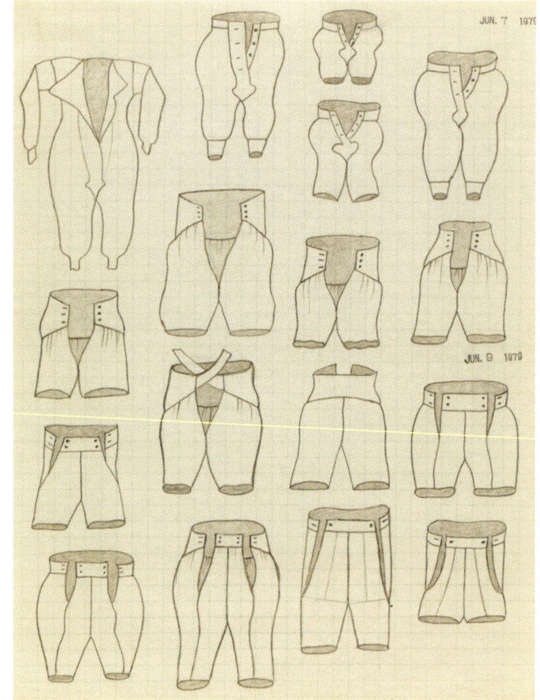

artists, too, sought to express a liberated yet historically rooted identity. Later in the decade, Christina Ramberg (1946–1995) focused on female undergarments: *Untitled (Bloomers)* (1979; fig. 38) features a garment developed in the mid-nineteenth century to increase women's comfort and mobility. In several places the work is stamped "Jun. 7 1979" and "Jun. 9 1979" (likely the dates of the work's creation—its "birth"—reminiscent of a fraktur *Taufschein*), highlighting women's rights and well-being across time.

In the following decade, graffiti artists began to express a new urban identity. As they moved into distressed neighborhoods, they joined with disenfranchised and under-resourced communities, largely African-American and Latino. Jean-Michel Basquiat moved quickly from graffiti to the world of galleries and museums with profoundly expressive paintings that spoke of slavery, colonialism, and racism. Stripped of individuality and humanity, the skeletal figure in *Untitled* (1982; fig. 39) is alive with rage. Such personages recur in his work; Basquiat called them "warriors." Holding a hatchet in one hand and a sword in the other, this warrior wears a red mask—another icon in Basquiat's visual vocabulary.

FIG. 37 (LEFT)
Andy Warhol, *Cecil Beaton's Feet*, 1961. Black ink on buff wove paper, 16¾ x 13⅞ in.
PHILADELPHIA MUSEUM OF ART: THE HENRY P. MCILHENNY COLLECTION IN MEMORY OF FRANCES P. MCILHENNY, 1982. © 2015 THE ANDY WARHOL FOUNDATION FOR THE VISUAL ARTS, INC. / ARTISTS RIGHTS SOCIETY (ARS), NEW YORK

FIG. 38 (RIGHT)
Christina Ramberg, *Untitled (Bloomers)*, 1979. Graphite on graph paper, 8½ x 11 in.
PENNSYLVANIA ACADEMY OF THE FINE ARTS, PHILADELPHIA. ART BY WOMEN COLLECTION, GIFT OF LINDA LEE ALTER

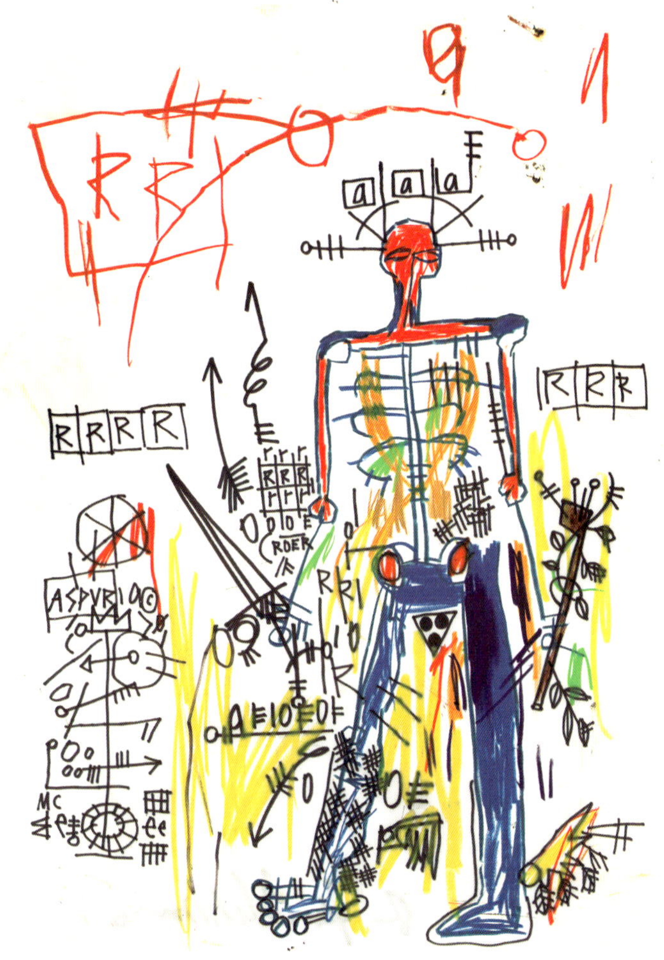

FIG. 39
Jean-Michel Basquiat, *Untitled*, 1982. Felt-tip pen and oilstick on paper, 30 x 22 in.

His headpiece conjures both the artist's famously sculptural hair and antennae—conduits for the energetic clusters of letters and symbols that flank the form. Although shuffled, the scarlet letters lacerating the composition are those of "warrior." Scrawled or in grids, Basquiat's seeming wordplay may be deadly serious. "Roar" thunders for itself. "Roer" is a game-hunting rifle used in southern Africa. "Roan" describes animal coloring: typically, an even mix of brown and white. Vocalized, "rrrr" sounds a warning growl.[1] Basquiat's friend and fellow graffitist Keith Haring (1958–1990) (who, incidentally, was born and raised in Pennsylvania Dutch Country) exuded a child's joy in creating and, amid the AIDS epidemic, addressed sexual identity and AIDS as social, personal, and political issues in graphic images and words (fig. 40).

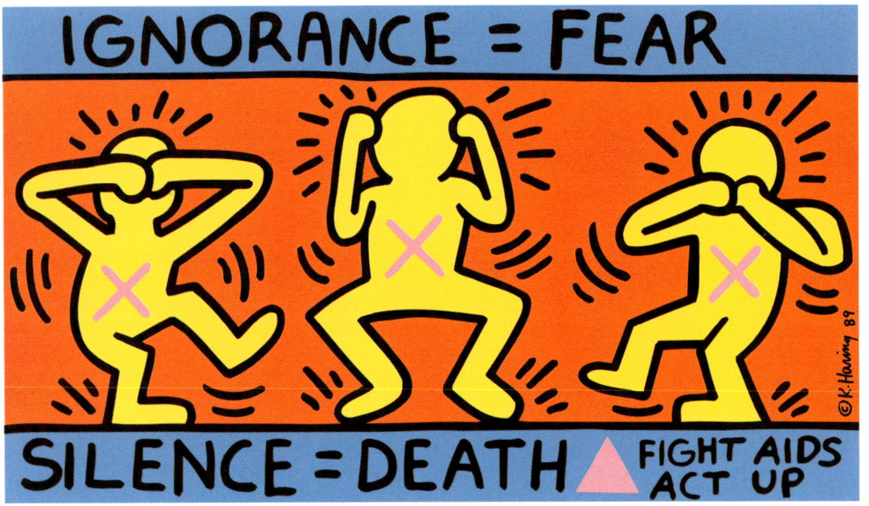

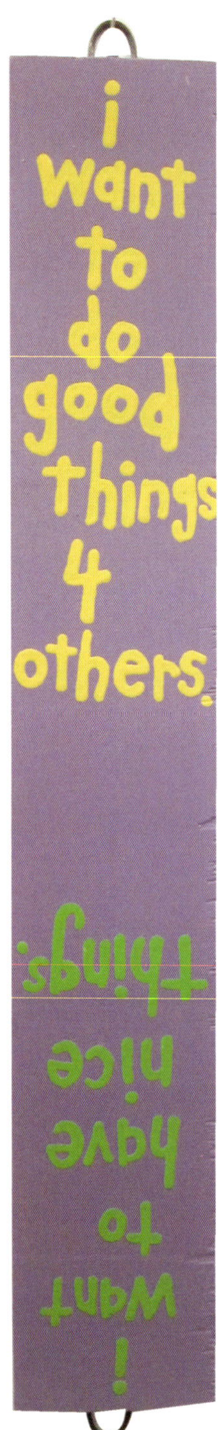

In the 1990s, a decade known even in its own time for a pervasive sense of irony in popular culture, artists' statements in word and image changed in tone. The art of Cary Leibowitz, a.k.a Candyass (b. 1963), addresses a breathtaking range of personal struggles and issues of individual, group, even national identity—appearance, queerness, Jewishness, inadequacy, Americana, character, social consciousness, race, popular culture, consumerism, modernism, and kitsch. His text-based paintings feature determinedly childlike lettering, which Leibowitz initially called "New American Calligraphy." What they say is mordant, self-effacing, and subversive, leavened with humor and a palpable sense of good-natured decency (fig. 41). Similarly, the text paintings of Sean Landers (b. 1962) are, typically, covered from edge to edge with the words of a stream-of-conscious, internal monologue that is alternately self-aggrandizing and self-questioning. They are raw, honest, overflowing with pathos—and funny. We cannot be sure whether they are autobiographical or imagined. This blurring and merging of fact and fantasy is underscored by the hybrid creatures that populate Landers's paintings. They fuse the human, animal, and mechanical worlds (fig. 42) and the realms of the grotesque and the adorable.

"Street Art" was and is an expression of the age-old instinct to claim a public space for oneself by marking it with graffiti, paired with political consciousness and the clarity of (often humorous) expression found in text-based art. Stephen Powers (b. 1968), first known by his

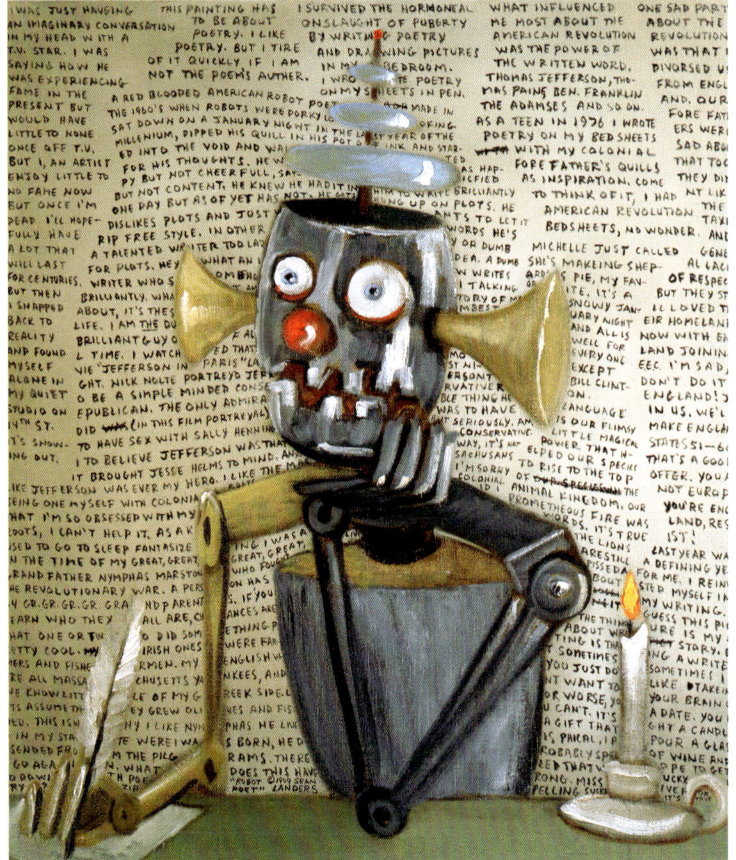

FIG. 40 (FAR LEFT)
Keith Haring, *Ignorance = Fear*, 1989. Offset-lithograph on glazed poster paper, 24 x 43¼ in.
© KEITH HARING FOUNDATION

FIG. 41 (LEFT)
Cary Leibowitz, *I Want To Do Good Things*, 1993. Latex on wood panel, 25¾ x 4¼ in.
COURTESY THE ARTIST AND INVISIBLE-EXPORTS, NEW YORK

FIG. 42 (RIGHT)
Sean Landers, *The Robot Poet*, 1999. Oil on linen, 30 x 26 in.
COURTESY THE ARTIST AND FRIEDRICH PETZEL GALLERY, NEW YORK

nom-de-graffiti, ESPO, long walked the thin line separating graffiti as illegal vandalism and commissioned public art. He is well known for highly visible, large-scale projects such as *A Love Letter to Brooklyn* (2011). Less known is his strong interest in his Pennsylvania German heritage. Evidence of this is a traditionally made redware-with-slip-decoration plate (1993; fig. 43) that he designed for Ari Saal Forman, his friend and partner in publishing *On the Go* magazine. A towering lightbulb marches the streetscape carrying a can of spray paint. Paraphrasing Gil Scott-Heron with wit, the plate reads, "The evolution will be live."

In the twenty-first century, the lineage that links these artists underpins the work of a group of contemporary artists that I will call Millennial Urban Rustics (MUR), who emerged at the turn of this century in spots spread wide across this continent and who share a certain longing for and ideal of community with the fraktur artists. Like fraktur, their

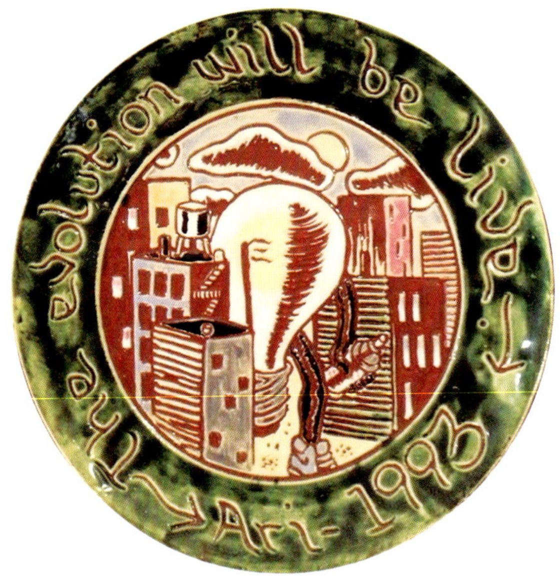

FIG. 43
Stephen Powers / ESPO, *Untitled*, 1993. Created at Long Family Potters, Phoenixville, Pennsylvania, under the supervision of master-potter Dorothy Long. Glazed earthenware with slip decoration; 8 in. diameter
COURTESY ARI SAAL FORMAN AND THE ARTIST

work combines words and images to express identity and memory. In response to the digital age, they create art that has the homespun, time-worn patina of folk art.

Most of the Millennial Urban Rustics emerged as members of informal and organized artists' collaboratives formed between 1995 and 2002 in San Francisco (the Mission School), Providence (Fort Thunder), Winnipeg (Royal Art Lodge), and Philadelphia (Space 1026). Almost all are art-school educated. Yet their art seemed to spring fully formed from a subculture of punk rock, skateboarding, surfing, and graffiti.

Under-resourced yet resourceful, and spurred by ecological concerns and punk's do-it-yourself ethos to remake, remodel, and recycle, MUR artists made their debut with paintings on flat and aggregated surfaces composed of found objects. Their images are quirky and folksy, their lettering eccentric, embellished, and always distinctive—like fraktur. Though spread from coast to coast, these artists know one another well, often collaborating and exhibiting together. They are a community of communities.

The sprawling wall-works of Barry McGee (b. 1966; fig. 44) are compositions of disparate items fit tightly together. McGee's human subjects are down-and-out urban men, depicted in subdued shades of black and white. By contrast, his abstract work looks like quilting-patterns-as-Op-art. The texts in McGee's work are bold and bright interpretations of the

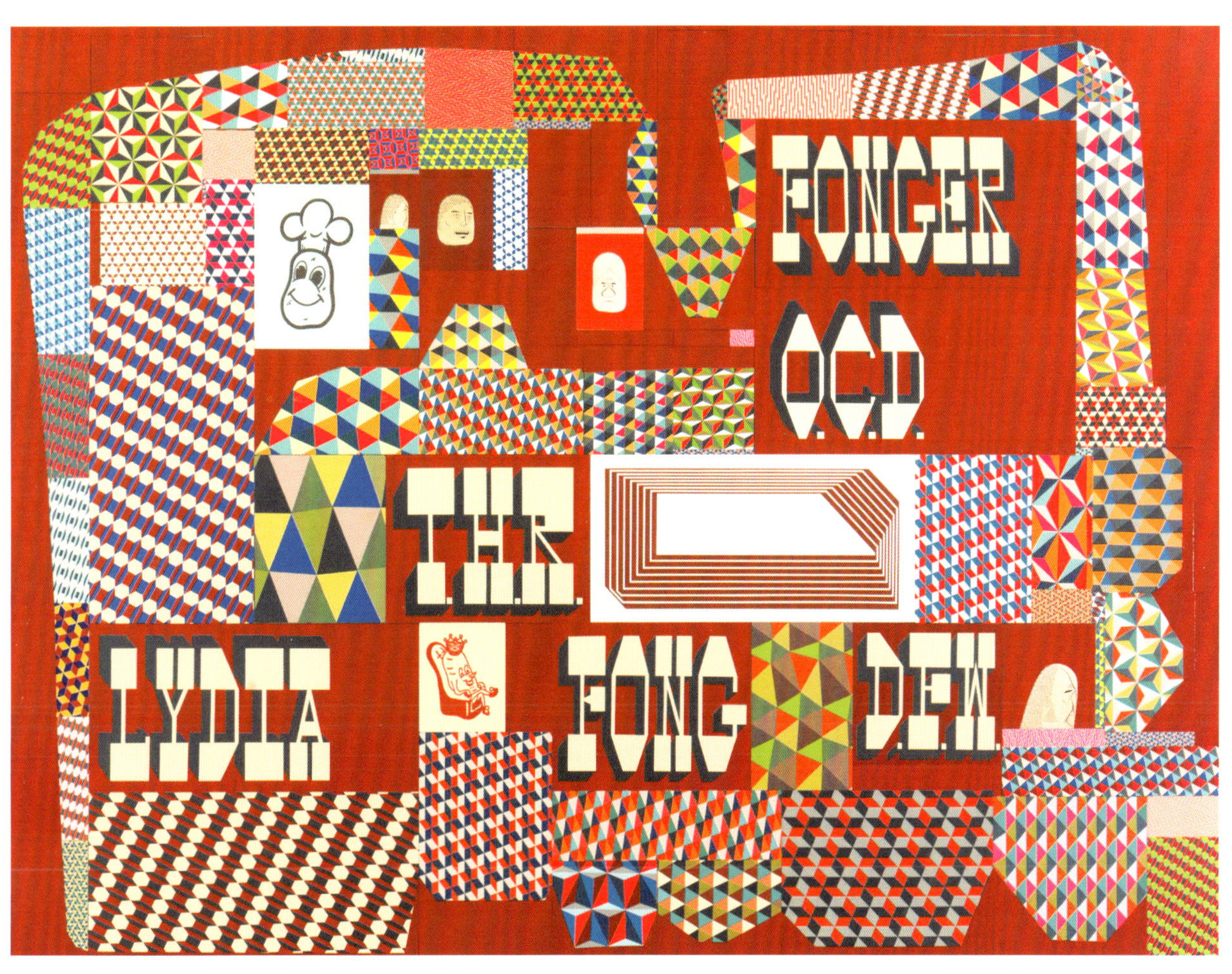

FIG. 44

Barry McGee, *Untitled*, 2013.
Acrylic on wood panel,
102 elements, 136½ x 180 in.

COURTESY THE ARTIST AND RATIO 3,
SAN FRANCISCO

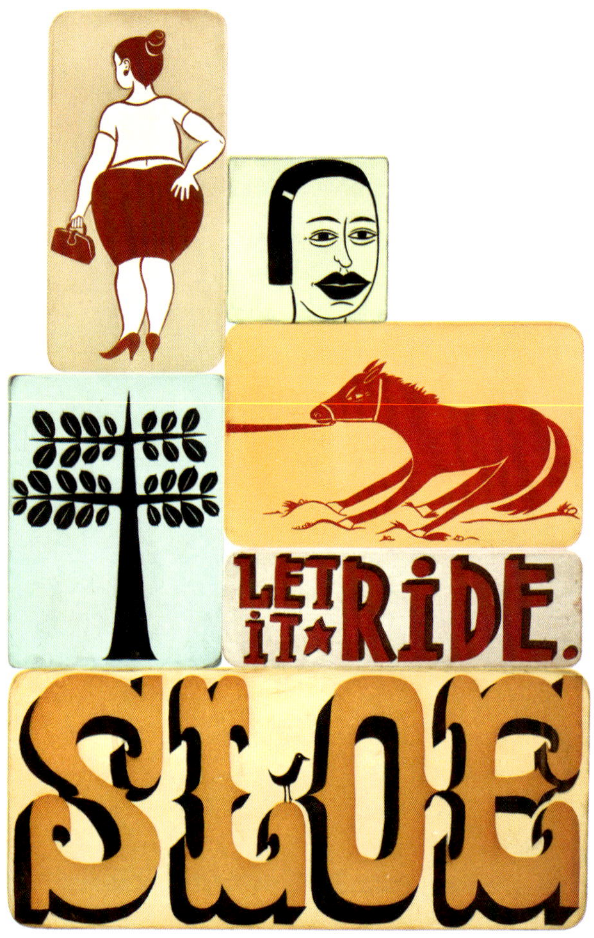

FIG. 45
Margaret Kilgallen, *Sloe*, 1998. Color, aquatint etching with sugarlift, 36 x 24½ in.
COURTESY THE ARTIST'S ESTATE AND RATIO 3, SAN FRANCISCO

graffiti aliases he uses: Ray Fong, Lydia Fong (McGee is half Chinese by descent), Twist, and the initials of the graffiti crews and side collaboration in which he's involved, DFW (Down for Whatever) and THR (The Harsh Reality), among others. By incorporating his graffiti personae into his clustered wall-works, McGee bridges his dual identity as a graffitist and oft-exhibited, and avidly collected, "gallery artist." There is a distinctly urban tension and a sense of melancholy in his work. He commemorates the San Francisco of his youth before the influx of digital dollars and the pre-modern world he never knew — one without consumerism and the related anxieties of urban life.

Margaret Kilgallen (1967–2001) was a painter with a passion for letter forms that she shared with McGee, her husband and frequent collaborator. Kilgallen responded to the coded messages and aliases of hobos

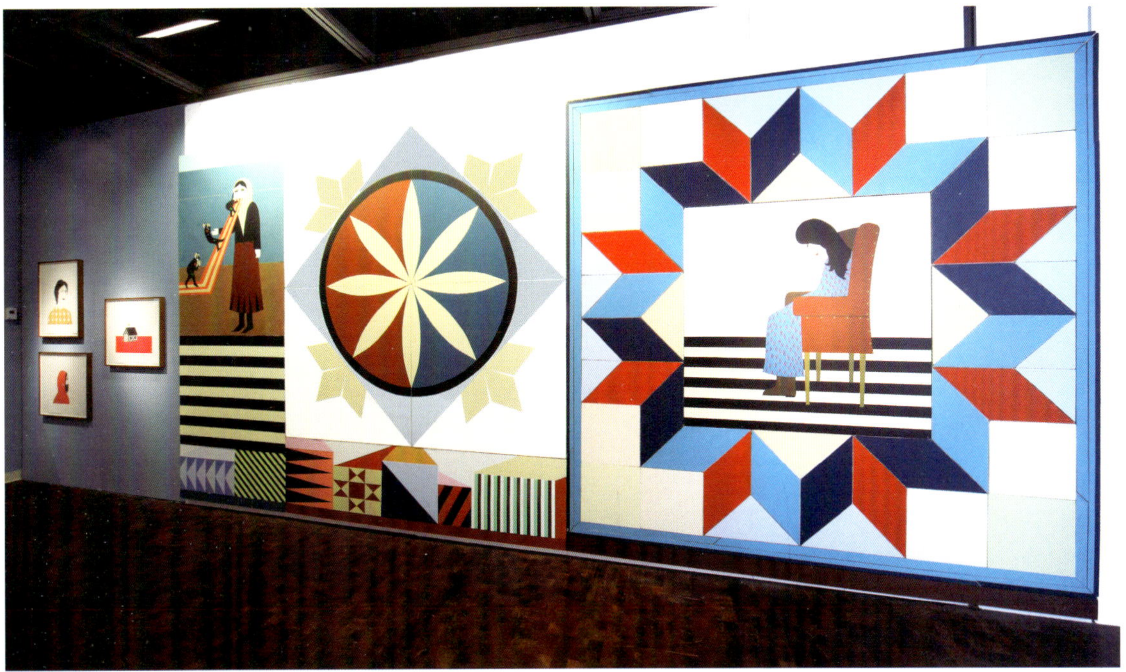

FIG. 46
Clare Rojas, installation view of the exhibition *We They, We They*, 2010, at the Museum of Craft and Folk Art, San Francisco
COURTESY THE ARTIST AND GALLERY PAULE ANGLIM, SAN FRANCISCO

and the music of Appalachia, especially its female musicians. Unassuming but self-reliant women dominate her figurative work. Recorded in Kilgallen's art are the names of revered female folk musicians, California place-names, and surf slang.[2] In the case of *Sloe* (fig. 45), Kilgallen's references include California-grown berries.

Raised in northern Maryland, Kilgallen and her family took day trips to the Pennsylvania Dutch Country, where she absorbed the visual culture of the area, quilt patterns in particular. Kilgallen painted on four-by-eight-foot sheets of plywood and large stretches of canvas, creating works that look like quilts writ large—"women's work" on a monumental scale. Her art is modern in its feminism, yet—like McGee's—evinces nostalgia. It "remembers" in words and pictures.

Clare Rojas (b. 1976) has been affiliated or associated with Fort Thunder, Space 1026, and the Mission School. While she is now exploring pure abstraction—an evolution seen in the work of other MUR artists—her previous expansive and celebrated body of work was highly figurative, narrative, and folk-art informed. Pennsylvania German aesthetics can be seen in Rojas's interpretations of hex-sign-like pinwheels and other starry, geometric shapes (fig. 46). They appear on their own and ward away trouble from simple white structures that suggest farmhouses. Quilting is echoed and is transformed in Rojas's abstract compositions, her approach to installation, and in the making of some of the hex signs and farmhouses: Rojas pieced them together from wood cut into squares, rectangles, and triangles.

Rojas's figures are most often women who exude competence and strength. Typically, they appear to be from an earlier time. They reflect the artist's rejection of "official" history as written, with women rendered all but invisible. The contributions of determined, resourceful, stoic pioneer women—for one example—are not part of the long-accepted syllabus that teaches of America's expansion westward. Rojas gives such women pride of place—their due place—in the American and human story.

Philadelphia born and bred, Jim Houser (b. 1973) is a visual artist with a poet's sensibility whose work explores the relationship between the look, sound, and meaning of words and the things they represent. His painted words suggest snippets from overheard conversations or an inner monologue of his own. Houser creates enveloping environments by painting directly on walls, ceilings, and floors, then layering on clusters of paintings, drawings, and objects that he has transformed with paint: sneakers, basketballs, flowerpots, skateboard decks. *This Place Is Ours* (2005; fig. 47) refers to a strip of Nantucket beach where the late Rebecca Westcott (1976–2004), Jim's wife and fellow artist, was raised and where her ashes were scattered.

Also a Philadelphia native, Shelley Spector (b. 1960) finds, gathers, and sorts objects, then reassembles them in new contexts, imagining and reimagining the details of the American past and present. Her installation *Keep the Home Fires Burning* at the Philadelphia Museum of Art in 2015 was inspired by a large embroidery in the PMA collection: it was designed by folk art historian Frances Lichten (1889–1961) and embroidered by her mother, Cecelia, with the familiar Pennsylvania German motifs of birds, flowers, angels, and hearts. Completed in 1943, it was given to the museum after Lichten's death by Katherine Milhous, an artist and Lichten's companion of forty years. *Frances Loves Katherine* (2015;

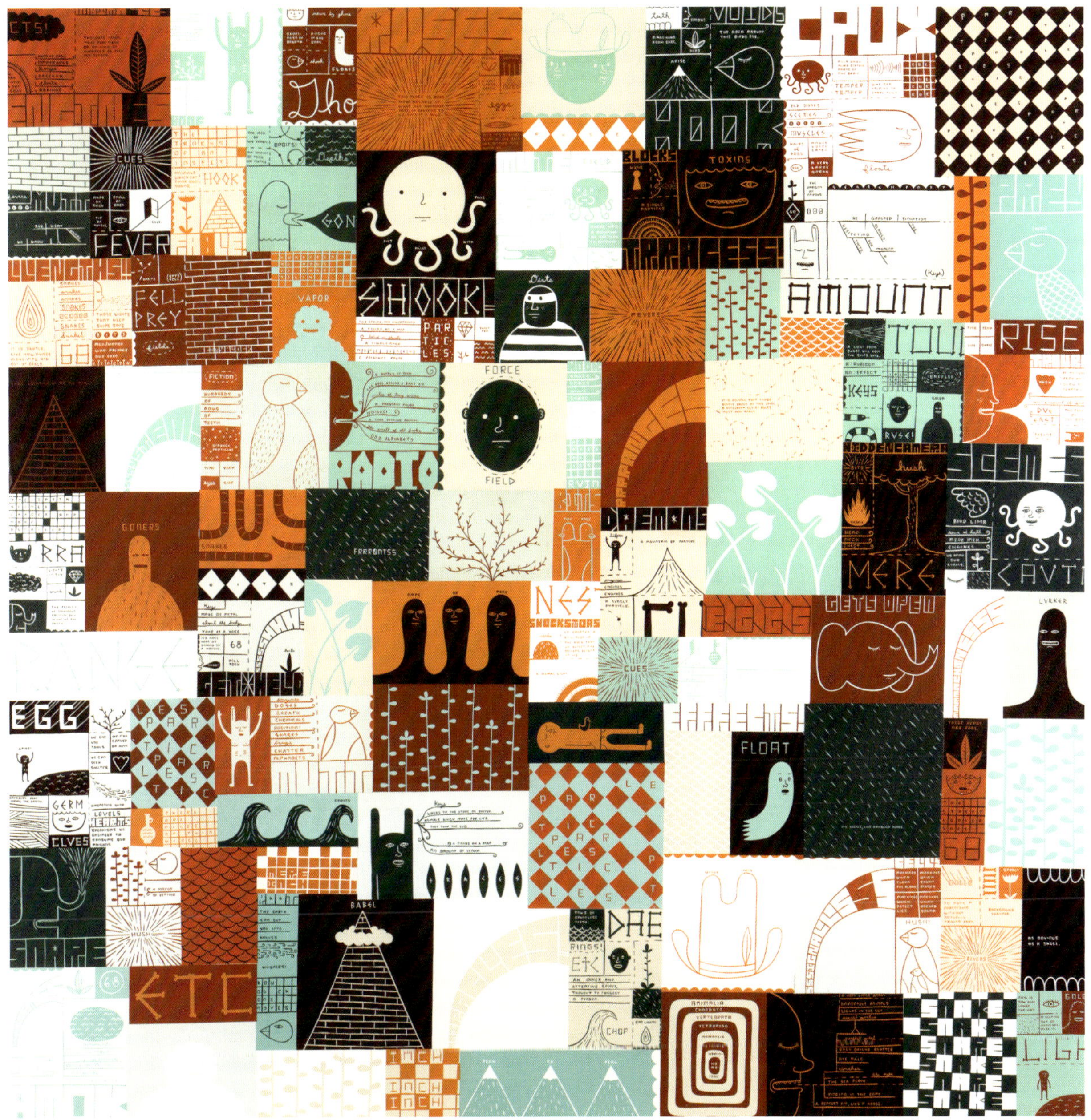

FIG. 47

Jim Houser, *This Place Is Ours*, 2005. Acrylic on paper collaged on canvas, 40 x 40 in.

PENNSYLVANIA ACADEMY OF THE FINE ARTS, PHILADELPHIA. CONTEMPORARY ART DEVELOPMENT FUND

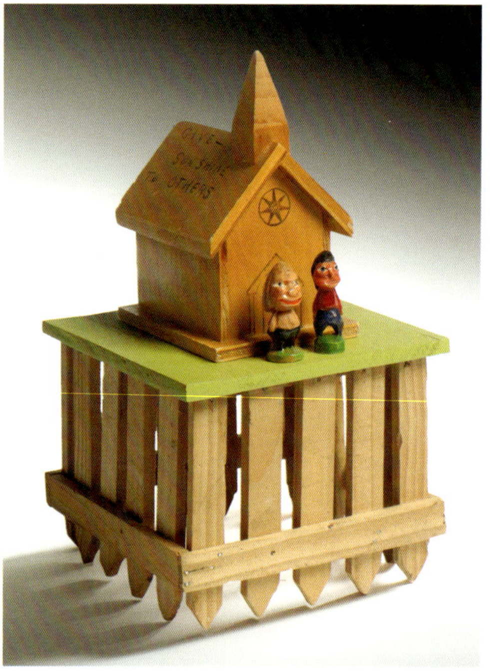

FIG. 48
Shelley Spector, *Frances Loves Katherine*, 2014. Wood and paint, 6 x 9 x 6 in.
COURTESY THE ARTIST

fig. 48) makes material Spector's imagining of the life they shared. "Give Sunshine to Others" is writ large on the tiny cottage roof.

Born and raised in New York state and a longtime resident of Philadelphia, Joy Feasley (b. 1966) blends nature, the supernatural, and memory. *Memorial Picture* (2007; fig. 49) was inspired by a trip to the Ephrata Cloister—once the settlement of a separatist sect that included America's first fraktur artists. Inside the blooms of this potted plant are the curvaceous outlines of fraktur letters—the initials of people dear to Feasley but whom she hadn't seen in some time and was remembering.

The surfaces upon which Isaac Tin Wei Lin (b. 1976) paints include photographs; life-size blow-ups of cartoon-like cats he's drawn; art-ready paper, canvas, and panels; and objects of the home and the street. He covers these surfaces with dense, fluid but robust, precisely drawn, and graphically engaging marks that appear to be the letters of an unknown language written in exquisite calligraphy. These shapes hold the power and promise of communication, but they are complete abstractions, creations of Isaac's imagination. Chinese American, Lin is the son of parents born in China. He has witnessed the challenges of those assimilating into a new culture while grappling with its language.

Lin has described the meditative quality of his extraordinary mark-making. One wonders whether it, in addition, offers the unusual experience of creating "letters" that may be appreciated as shapes but not read—what we do when encountering alphabets completely different from our own.

Lin explores and honors his family and its history in his work. *Black Water* (2013; fig. 50) shows two smiling women sitting on what appears to be a concrete ledge overlooking an indeterminate landscape—the background is obscured, to mesmerizing effect, by Lin's calligraphy. A narrative is suggested, though one as open-ended as the "meaning" of Lin's marks.

Also noteworthy are contemporary artists of Pennsylvania German descent who were born and bred in the Dutch Country, whose work overtly reflects the aesthetic aspects of their ethnic heritage.

A practicing Mennonite, Philadelphia-based artist Tim Gierschick II (b. 1976) makes paintings, drawings, and sculpture, incorporating traditional Pennsylvania German tools and techniques and commonplace

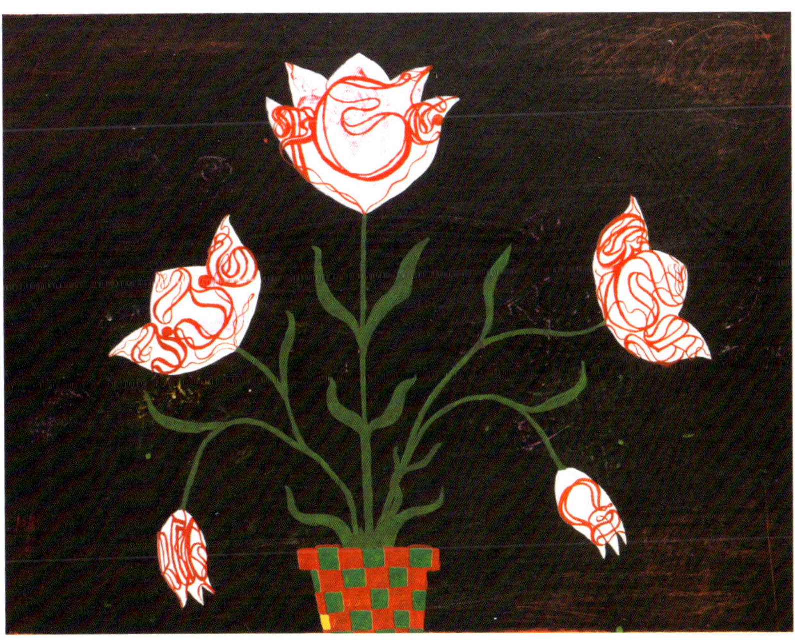

FIG. 49
Joy Feasley, *Memorial Picture*, 2007. Vinyl paint on medium-density overlay plywood, 15 x 20 in.
COURTESY THE ARTIST AND LOCKS GALLERY, PHILADELPHIA

FIG. 50
Isaac Tin Wei Lin, *Black Water*, 2013. Ink on photograph, 12 x 16 in.
COURTESY THE ARTIST AND FLEISHER/OLLMAN, PHILADELPHIA

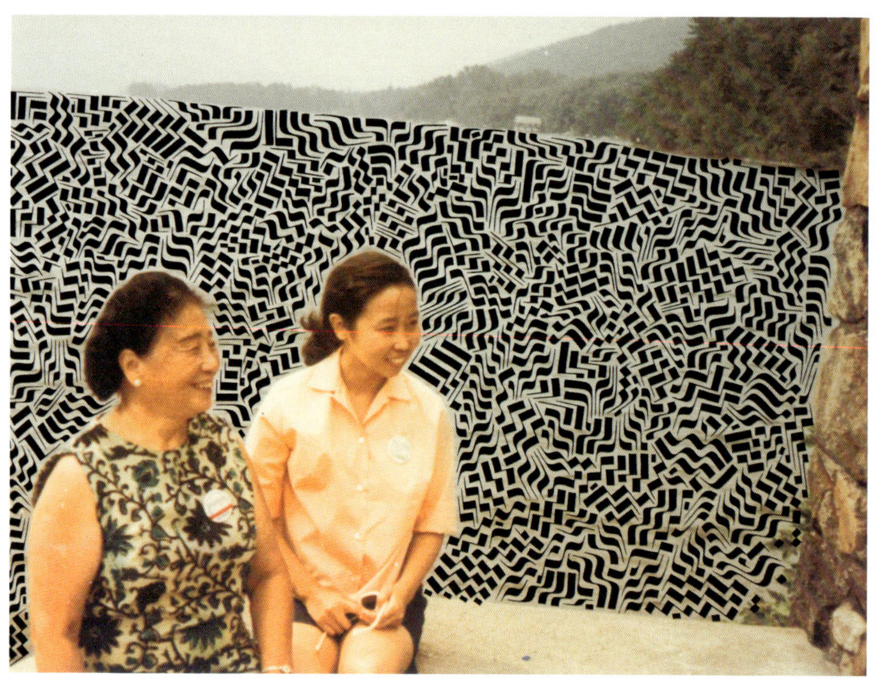

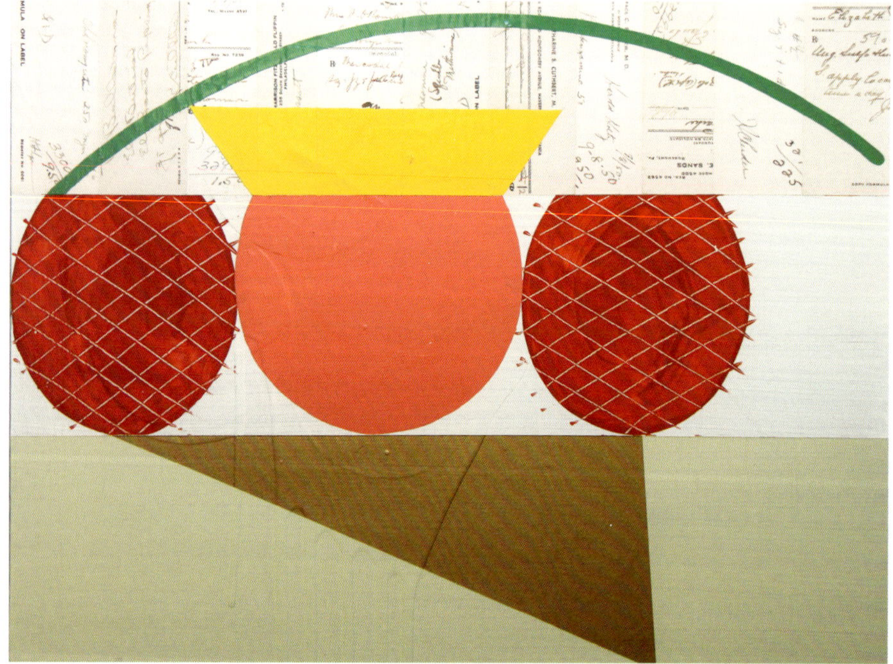

FIG. 51
Timothy Gierschick II, *Goldpot*, 2010. House paint, enamels, and collage on panel, 15 x 20 in.
COURTESY THE ARTIST

materials such as found wood and house and sign paint. In describing *Goldpot* (2010; fig. 51), Gierschick says he sees it as a "self-conscious, post-modern version of the stylized forms found in fraktur: flowers, landscapes, architecture—and household objects, like pots. My use of abstracted and stylized forms is directly linked to that of traditional fraktur artists. They, innately, saw a link between living life and representing it. So do I." The found, lettered paper at the top of *Goldpot* has no direct relationship to the work's images. Such textual elements are common in Gierschick's art. They converse with him as he forms the composition, and he sees them as points of discussion (internal or aloud) for the viewer.

Jerome Hershey (b. 1950) has Swiss-German ancestry in Pennsylvania that can be traced back to 1712 or earlier. Hershey, based in Lancaster, was taught to appreciate traditional Pennsylvania German craft and art traditions by his grandparents, parents, aunts and uncles, and cousins. Among his family's heirlooms was the celebrated "Huber Schrank" (1779), a masterpiece of Pennsylvania German cabinetmaking (a *Schrank* is a cupboard or wardrobe), now in the collection of the Philadelphia Museum of Art.

Hershey uses words to create abstractions. In *Interesting and Irresistible* (2010; fig. 52) and other examples of his "Word" paintings, the words of the title are repeated, layered, and fragmented. Hershey explains, "Repeated over and over, the words become purposefully illegible, serendipitous rhythms of lines and colors in transition."

Dennis Stephan (b. 1947), also based in Lancaster, retired from his graphic-design practice in 2011 with plans to devote more time to a passion: creating new fraktur that, while made to commemorate contemporary life-cycle events, was guided by historic examples and made with period-appropriate instruments, materials, and techniques. Since then, Stephan has become one of the most respected and sought-after makers of contemporary, yet traditional, fraktur. Recently, Stephan began to make art that is directly informed by fraktur but entirely new in appearance and process—his own creative expression. *Crossover* (2015; fig. 53) is a "poster size" twenty-four-by-twenty-inch giclée print inspired by

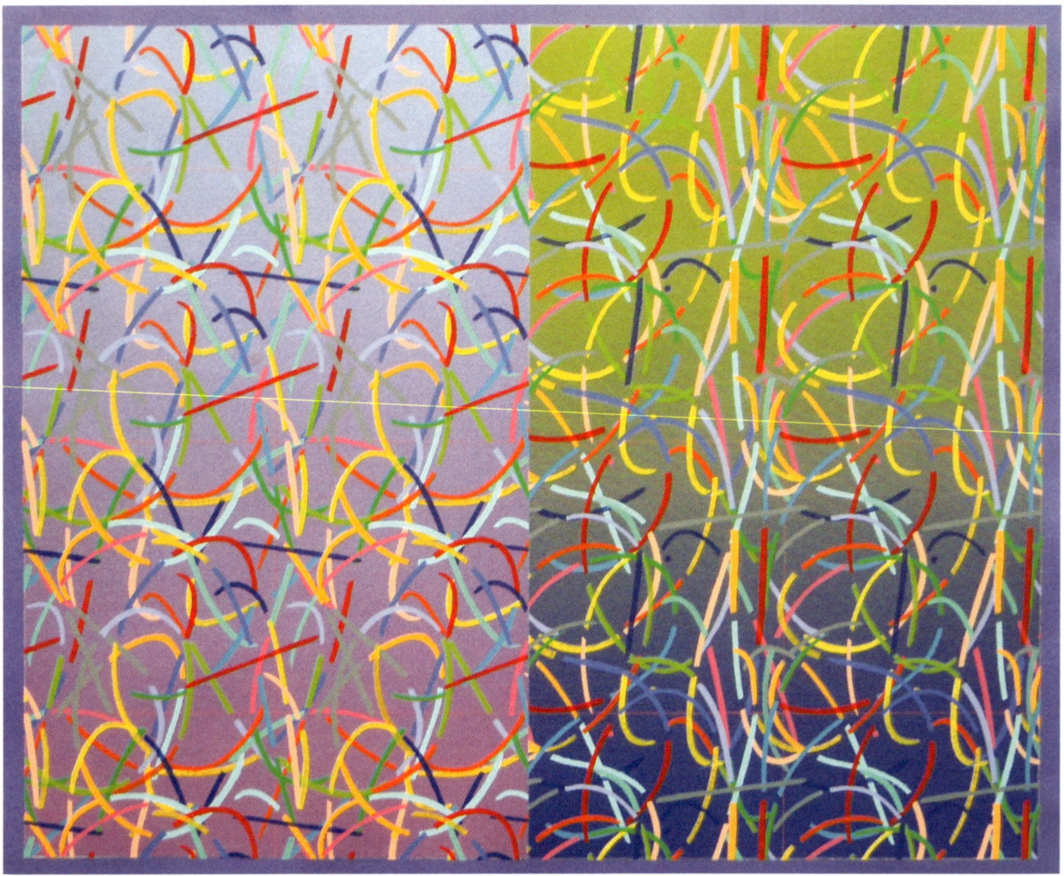

FIG. 52
Jerome Hershey, *Interesting and Irresistible*, 2010.
Acrylic on paper, 25½ x 32 in.
COURTESY THE ARTIST

the "poster portraits" created by Stephan's fellow Lancaster artist, the American early Modernist Charles Demuth (see page 49). In his contemporary work, Stephan isolates decorative motifs found in fraktur, such as the pinwheel, and enlarges them to emphasize their graphic power. Fraktur's "fractured" lettering is broken further into portions of single or intersecting letters, then "writ large," allowing the viewer to appreciate them as graceful abstractions.

Douglas Witmer (b. 1971), now a Philadelphia resident, was born and raised in a Mennonite community that valued and emphasized "plainness"—unadorned function for things material, humility, and group-mindedness for the self. Ultimately, this plainness is a spiritual imperative—it honors the divine by deferring to it. Witmer is a painter of abstraction that is "pure"—it does not reference the perceived world. Viewed in groups, his paintings evoke an artist exploring, with intent, the infinite possibilities presented by varying shape, color, and surface. Alone, a painting by Witmer is "visual" enough to engage eye and mind, yet "plain" enough to allow the viewer to project her or his perceptions, to meditate, or simply to be present in the experience of seeing.

Witmer paints with the viewer in mind. He says, "I have always had the desire that my work be 'useful' for others. This comes out of my Mennonite upbringing, where image-making was meant to function as decoration or 'serve' as an illustration of something else." In his art, Witmer expresses himself while honoring the practical Mennonite worldview: it is "useful" investigation that serves others by providing moments of clarity and focus.

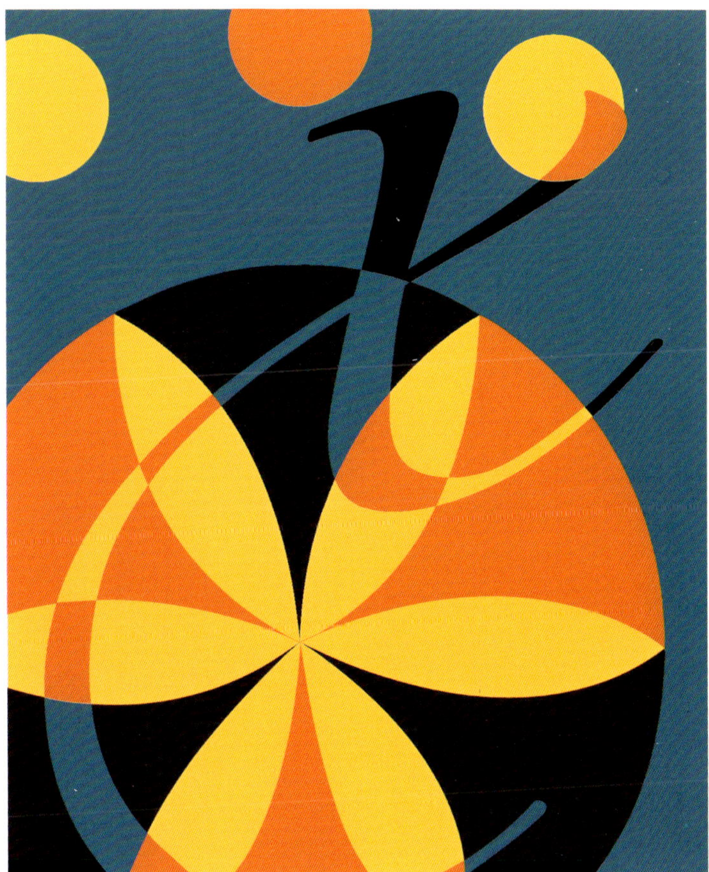

FIG. 53
Dennis Stephan, *Crossover*, 2015. Giclée print, 24 x 20 in.
COURTESY THE ARTIST

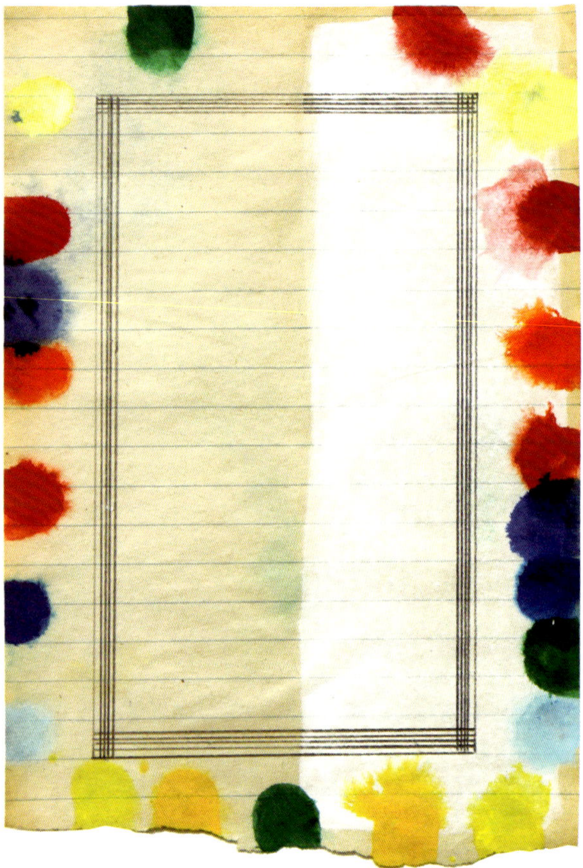

FIG. 54
Douglas Witmer, *School Papers (2013–1)*, 2013. Mixed media on found paper, 9 x 6 in.
PRIVATE COLLECTION, ENGLAND; COURTESY THE ARTIST

In *School Papers (2013–1)* (2013; fig. 54), Witmer maintains the purity of his abstraction while introducing elements that invoke the "fancy" and narrative/documentary nature of fraktur. On a timeworn sheet of ruled paper, Witmer has drawn a rectangle, a frame—a graphic device common to fraktur and other forms of illustration. Surrounding it are brightly colored splotches of paint that—like the "school paper" itself—recall childhood. These humble materials and their modest presentation evince joy, recalling for all when we first partook in the human ability to create.

In the end, art is always communication. Fraktur artists documented events, capturing their own time, place, and people for posterity. Unlike fraktur, words and identity in contemporary art are not always straightforward. They may be, or appear to be, random or deliberately ambiguous. Nonetheless, these artworks speak and encourage replies—they offer icebreakers in the conversation between artist, object, and viewer.[3]

NOTES

1 See Fred Hoffman, *Jean-Michel Basquiat Drawing: Work from the Schorr Family Collection* (New York: Acquavella Galleries and Rizzoli, 2014). Additional thanks to Mr. Hoffman for insights about Basquiat's "warrior" imagery in an e-mail to the author on March 23, 2015.

2 See Alex Baker, "Matokie Lives," in *Margaret Kilgallen: In the Sweet Bye and Bye* (Los Angeles: Roy and Edna Disney/CalArts Theater, 2005), 58–71.

3 Thanks to Timothy Gierschick II for noting that text in art—regardless of its content—inspires thought and discussion. Timothy Gierschick II, e-mail to the author, February 12, 2015.

Matthew F. Singer is senior writer for the Philadelphia Museum of Art, a curator at the Philadelphia Museum of Jewish Art, and a doctoral candidate in American Studies at Pennsylvania State University. His writings have appeared in publications for museums and galleries as well as DINOSAUR, Modernism, The Magazine Antiques, Veranda, *and other periodicals.*

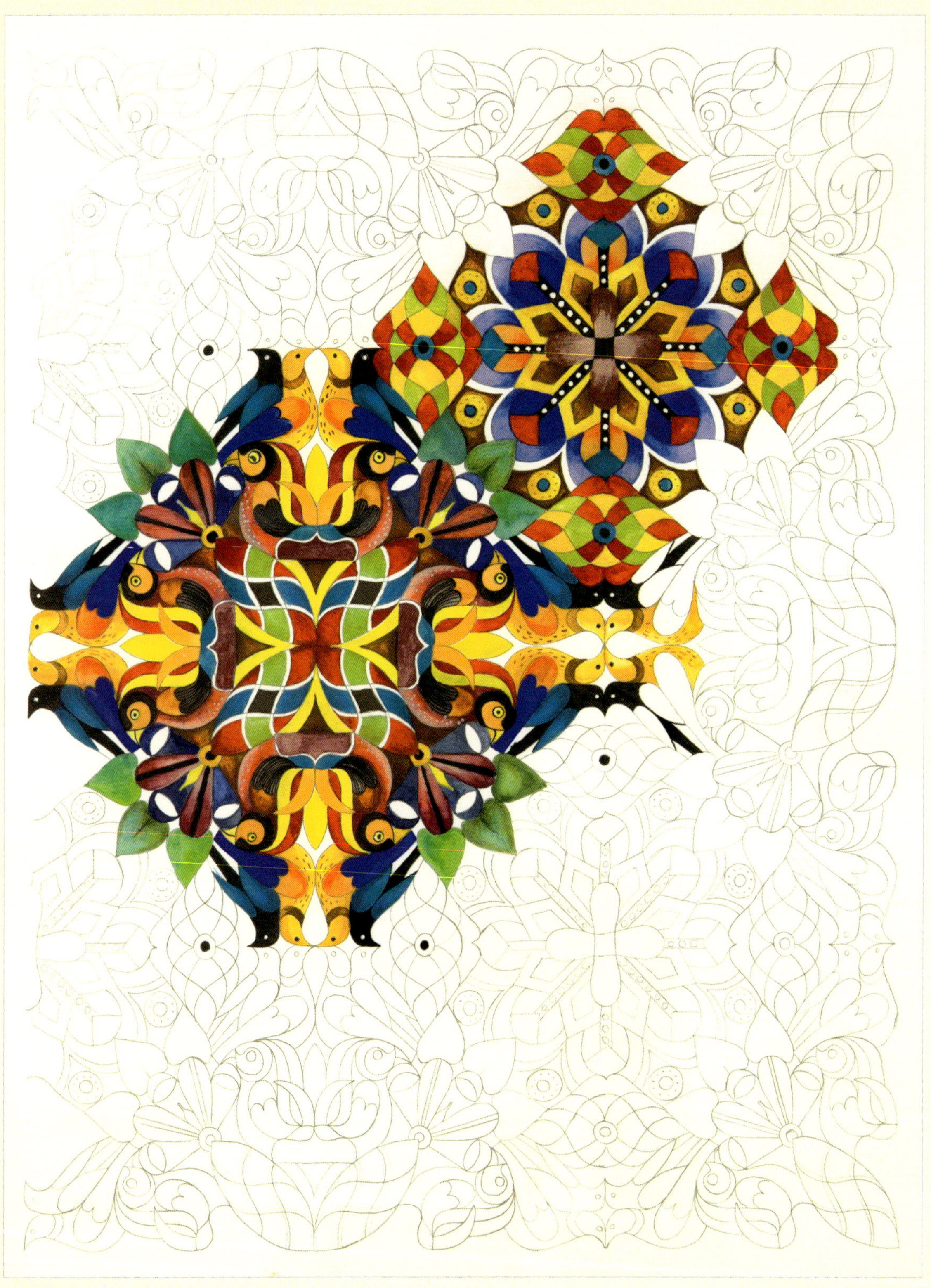

JUDITH TANNENBAUM

CONNECTING PRESENT TO PAST: CONTEMPORARY ARTISTS WITH LINKS TO FRAKTUR

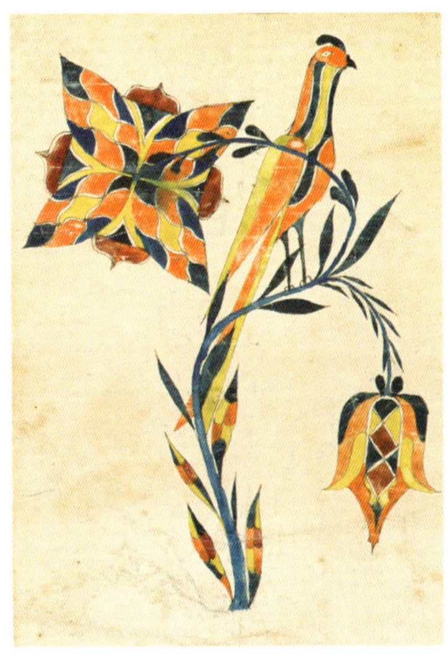

FIG. 55 (LEFT)
Marian Bantjes, *Pennsylvania Fraktur Pattern*, 2015. Watercolor and pencil crayon on watercolor paper, 22 x 15 in.
COURTESY THE ARTIST

FIG. 56 (ABOVE)
Drawing (bird on flower). Pennsylvania, c. 1830. Watercolor on wove paper, 7⅝ x 5⅞ in.
FREE LIBRARY OF PHILADELPHIA

We all grew up with the adage "a picture is worth a thousand words," but perhaps it's a false dichotomy to pit language against visual images. Art that inseparably links text and image may be more the rule than the exception throughout art history. East Asia (China, Japan, Korea, and other states) boasts centuries of marvelous scrolls and screens that superbly balance pictorial and written elements. Similarly, medieval Christian manuscripts such as books of hours, created for private prayer and devotion, and Mughal illuminated manuscripts from the Indian subcontinent dating back to the sixteenth century are profoundly beautiful and moving for the way in which they merge written and pictorial modes to create remarkably detailed and absorbing narratives. One thinks back even farther to Egyptian tomb paintings, where figure drawings coexist with hieroglyphics, and to Mayan and Aztec codices. Clearly, this is not a new phenomenon, nor is it limited to particular civilizations or cultures.

More recently, in Western European and American art, the juxtaposition of words and images has waxed and waned. Cubism, Dada, Surrealism, Pop, and Conceptual Art in the twentieth century include numerous artworks featuring text, but this approach was more of a rarity in the mid- and late nineteenth century, when Realism, Impressionism, and post-Impressionism predominated.

How and why do visual artists incorporate letters and words into their work, and when do writers choose to illustrate their texts with images and pictures or use text for its visual qualities? (Think of Jonathan Safran Foer's 2005 novel, *Extremely Loud and Incredibly Close*, which features "visual writing," blank pages, and a flipbook of photographs, as a good example.) Where does Pennsylvania German fraktur fit into this picture, and what is its artistic legacy? Faced with the challenge of choosing contemporary artists whose work resonates with eighteenth- and nineteenth-century Pennsylvania German fraktur, I focused on two characteristics of the genre: first, the coexistence and balance of the old German script and the decorative symbols with which it is embellished; second, but no less important, its character as a type of folk art. Of the seven contemporary artists in the exhibition *Word & Image*, some connect more directly with the idea of writing, whereas others riff on folk genres, and several do both.

MARIAN BANTJES (b. 1963) began her professional career as a typesetter and type designer. After spending ten years designing corporate identities and other communication materials, Bantjes decided to concentrate on work that is "highly personal, obsessive, and sometimes just plain weird."[1] She is a well-known figure in the ornamental movement, which has become prominent in design during the past decade. Bantjes embraces an ornate baroque style, but her sources and references range widely—from traditional Islamic and African art to twentieth-century Modernism. Beneath the fluid, organic look of her work is what the artist describes as "its underlying structure and formality."[2] Virtuosic patterns are applied in playful, inventive ways, as evidenced in three new drawings Bantjes made especially for the Philadelphia exhibition. Ranging from modernist abstraction to stylized birds and flowers and other Pennsylvania German folk motifs, these drawings reflect the artist's keen observation of traditional fraktur in the Free Library's collection (figs. 55, 56).

Bantjes's subject matter in other works ranges widely: in *My Dear, Can We Work Together* (2007; fig. 57), she copied the text verbatim from a spam email, a so-called Nigerian inheritance scam letter that came to her via the Internet, and transformed it into an imaginatively embellished document with a number of colors and styles of type; *Lost Child* (2014; fig. 59), a simpler composition in needlepoint, is made with hair from My Little Pony toys. Although these two works look very different, they both connect to

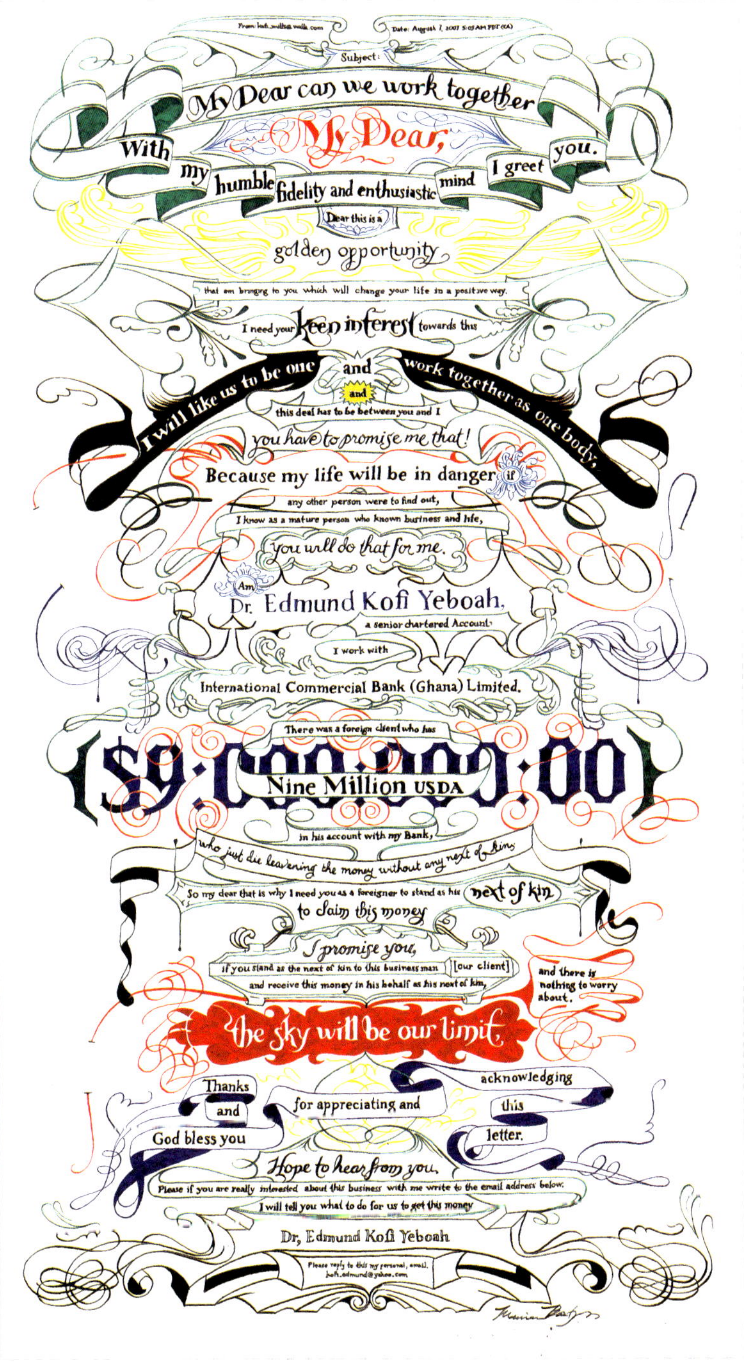

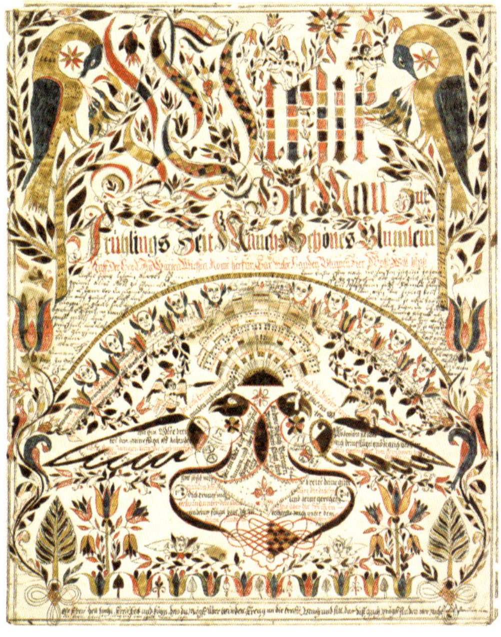

FIG. 57 (LEFT)

Marian Bantjes, *My Dear, Can We Work Together*, 2007. Pen and ink on paper, 22½ x 15 in.

COURTESY THE ARTIST

FIG. 58 (ABOVE)

Religious text. Bucks or Montgomery County, Pennsylvania, 1817. Watercolor and ink on laid paper, 15⅞ x 13 in.

FREE LIBRARY OF PHILADELPHIA

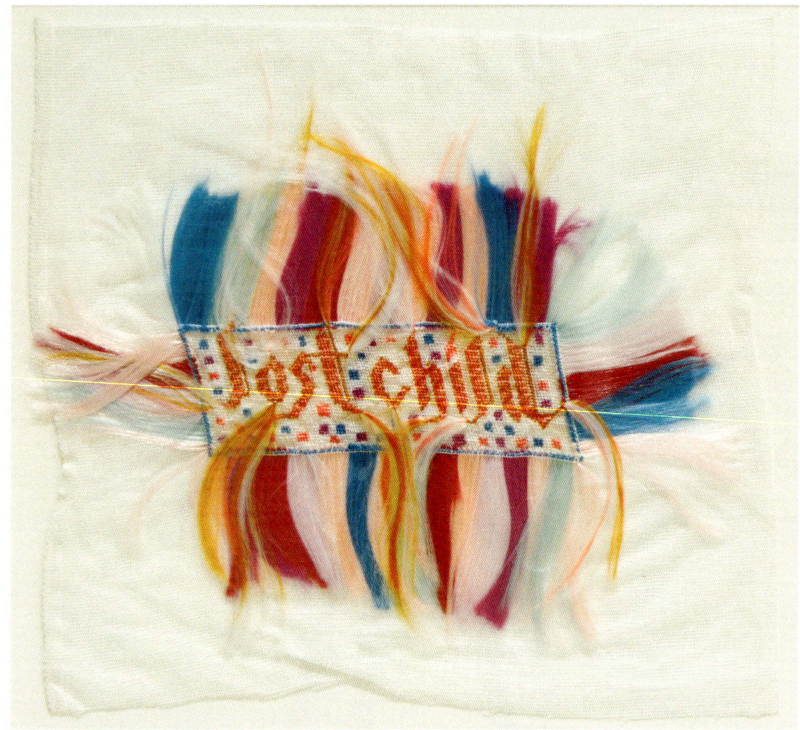

FIG. 59
Marian Bantjes, *Lost Child*, 2014. Needlepoint with synthetic hair from My Little Pony figures, 18 x 20 in.
COURTESY THE ARTIST

popular culture in our own time and demonstrate a sharp awareness of serious issues that underlie mass marketing and social media.

Because of her expertise with typefaces and graphic design, Bantjes was invited to design the graphic identity for *Framing Fraktur* (see front cover). The challenge was to create a legible design that is simultaneously traditional and contemporary, an adaptable logo that would be strongly associated with fraktur but not be mistaken for it. She exceeded expectations by employing angled multicolor lettering framed by ornamental birds and flowers inspired by fraktur in a cheerful palette of blue, red, yellow, and green. Similar to the technique she observed in Pennsylvania German fraktur, Bantjes split basic letter strokes in two, sometimes overlapping them with a third color.

BOB AND ROBERTA SMITH (the pseudonym of Patrick Brill, b. 1963) sees art as a singularly important element in democratic life and believes that art and art education should be available to all. Much of his own art takes the form of painted signs, often made with found wood and other everyday materials (fig. 60; see also fig. 80)—from cookie sheets to a full-size foot- and headboard. By choosing such mundane materials, he asserts in the medium as well as the message that anything can be used to make art and everyone has the potential to be an artist.

Smith's humorous, provocative slogans painted in brightly colored letters resemble handmade signs by folk artists or sign painters. Despite this connection to traditional styles of lettering, the subject matter always relates to current art and politics, and the folksy look of the work may belie the artist's deep knowledge of history and art history. When invited to participate in this exhibition, Smith revealed that a principal inspiration for his word paintings goes back to his love for such historic documents as the Lindesfarne Gospels (c. 700) and the Book of Kells (c. 800), masterpieces of calligraphy and manuscript illumination, and the Magna Carta (1215), which established the foundation of British law.[3]

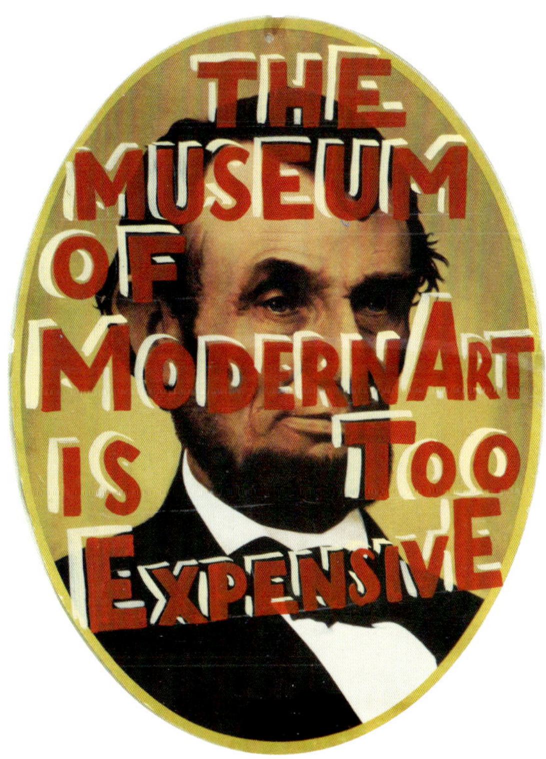

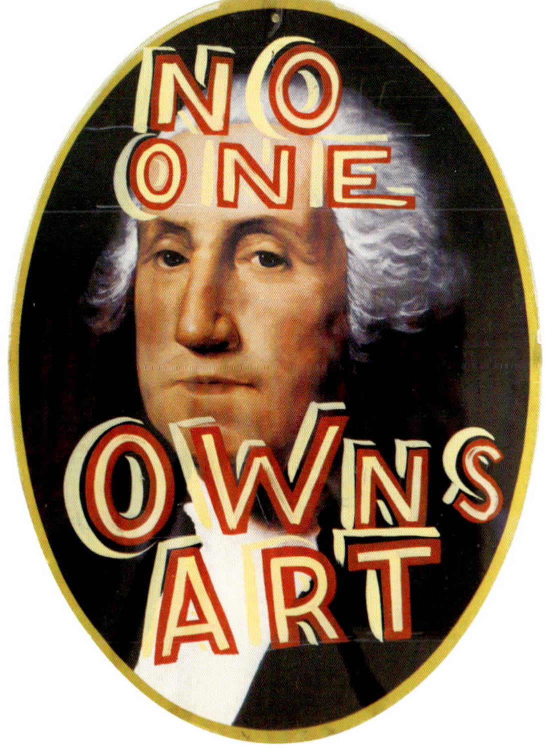

FIG. 60
Bob and Roberta Smith, *The Museum of Modern Art* and *No One Owns Art*, 2011. Enamel on found paper, 25 x 18½ in. (oval) each
COURTESY THE ARTIST AND PIEROGI GALLERY

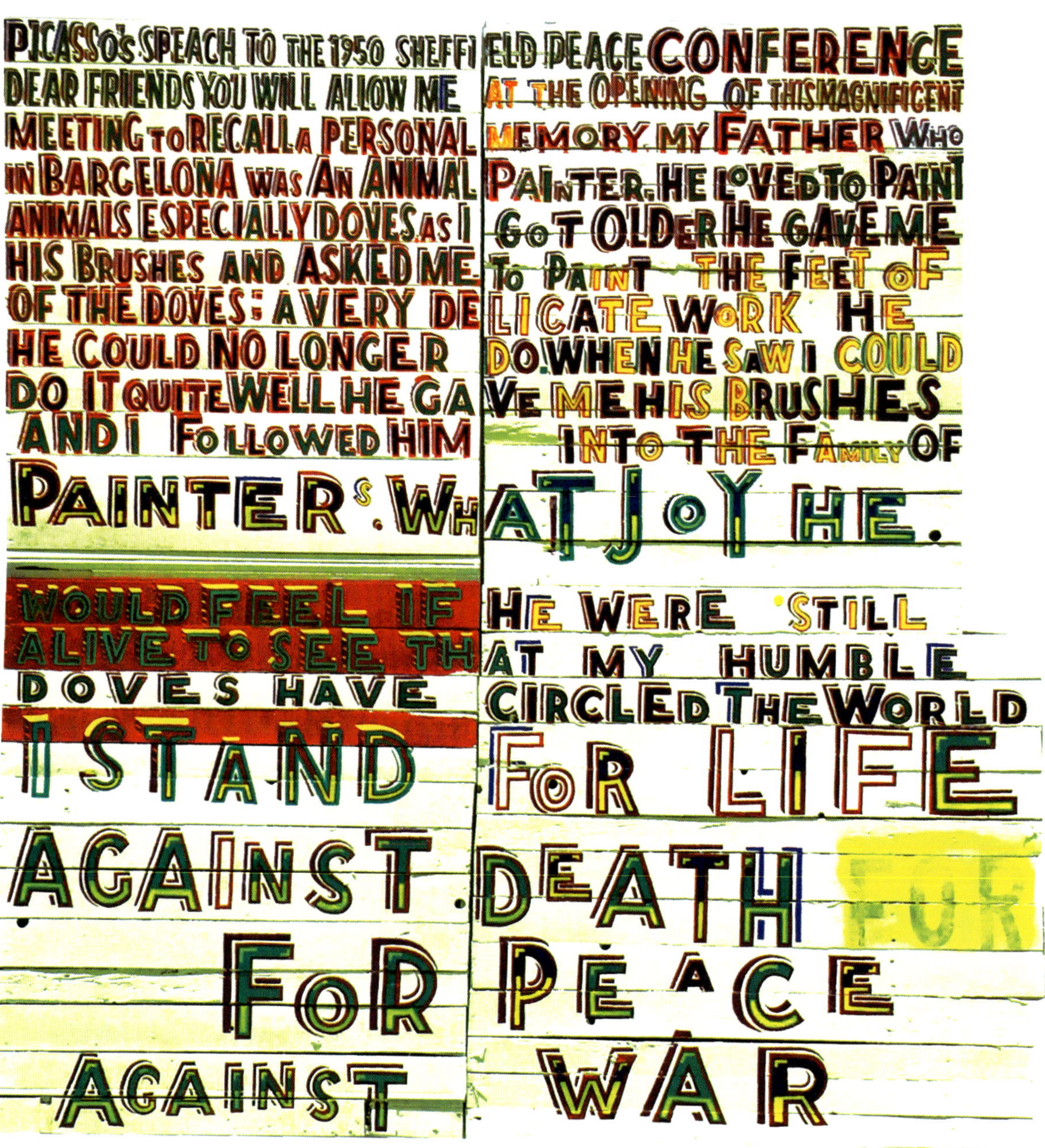

FIG. 61

Bob and Roberta Smith, *Picasso's Speech to the 1950 Peace Congress*, 2012. Oil on found wood, 90 x 86¾ in.

COURTESY THE ARTIST

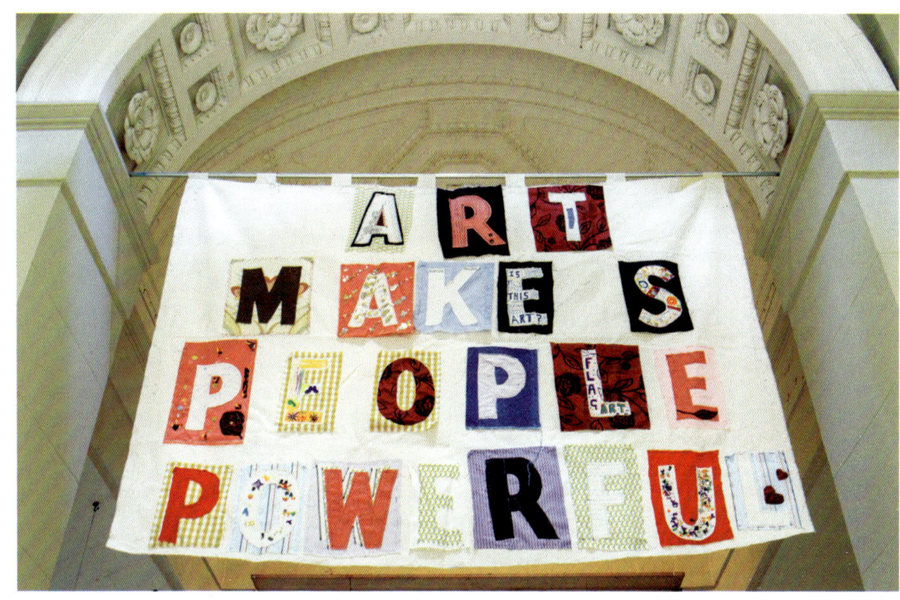

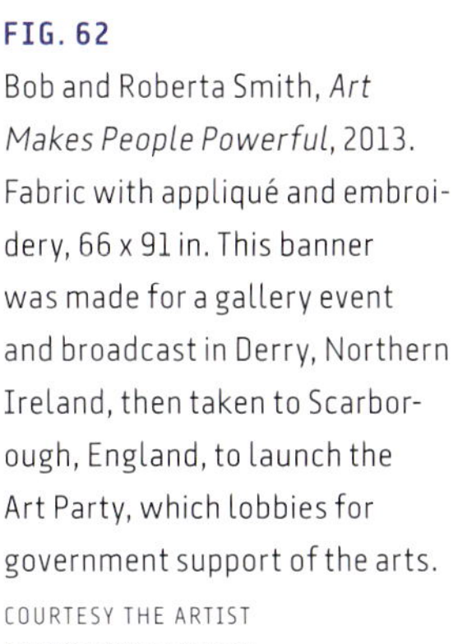

FIG. 62
Bob and Roberta Smith, *Art Makes People Powerful*, 2013. Fabric with appliqué and embroidery, 66 x 91 in. This banner was made for a gallery event and broadcast in Derry, Northern Ireland, then taken to Scarborough, England, to launch the Art Party, which lobbies for government support of the arts.
COURTESY THE ARTIST AND PIEROGI GALLERY

Some of Smith's paintings serve as manifestos, such as the *Letter to Michael Gove* (2011) and *Picasso's Speech to the 1950 Peace Congress* (2012; fig. 61). Smith manifests his own political activism in campaigns in both the United States and England. In conjunction with an exhibition at Pierogi Gallery's Boiler space in Brooklyn in 2011, he initiated the Art Party of the USA, which aims "to provide a creative yet critical discourse of hope in response to the Tea Party's discourse of austerity and despair."[4] In 2013 in Scarborough, England, he launched the Art Party, a loose grouping of progressive artists and organizations that lobbies the government on behalf of the arts (fig. 62). In addition to gallery shows, Smith presents radio and television broadcasts, music performances, and other multimedia events and has been the subject of several documentary films.

For **ANTHONY CAMPUZANO** (b. 1975), a newspaper headline about murders in Philadelphia, a song by Sister Sledge, a note from his mother to clean up his room, an Emily Dickinson poem, an encounter with underground actor Taylor Mead—all are fodder for word paintings and drawings, along with texts he makes up himself. Sometimes the words are big, bold, and easy to read, whereas in other compositions the dense repetition of letters or phrases and shifts in direction make the language more difficult to decipher. With small repeated hand gestures, he methodically

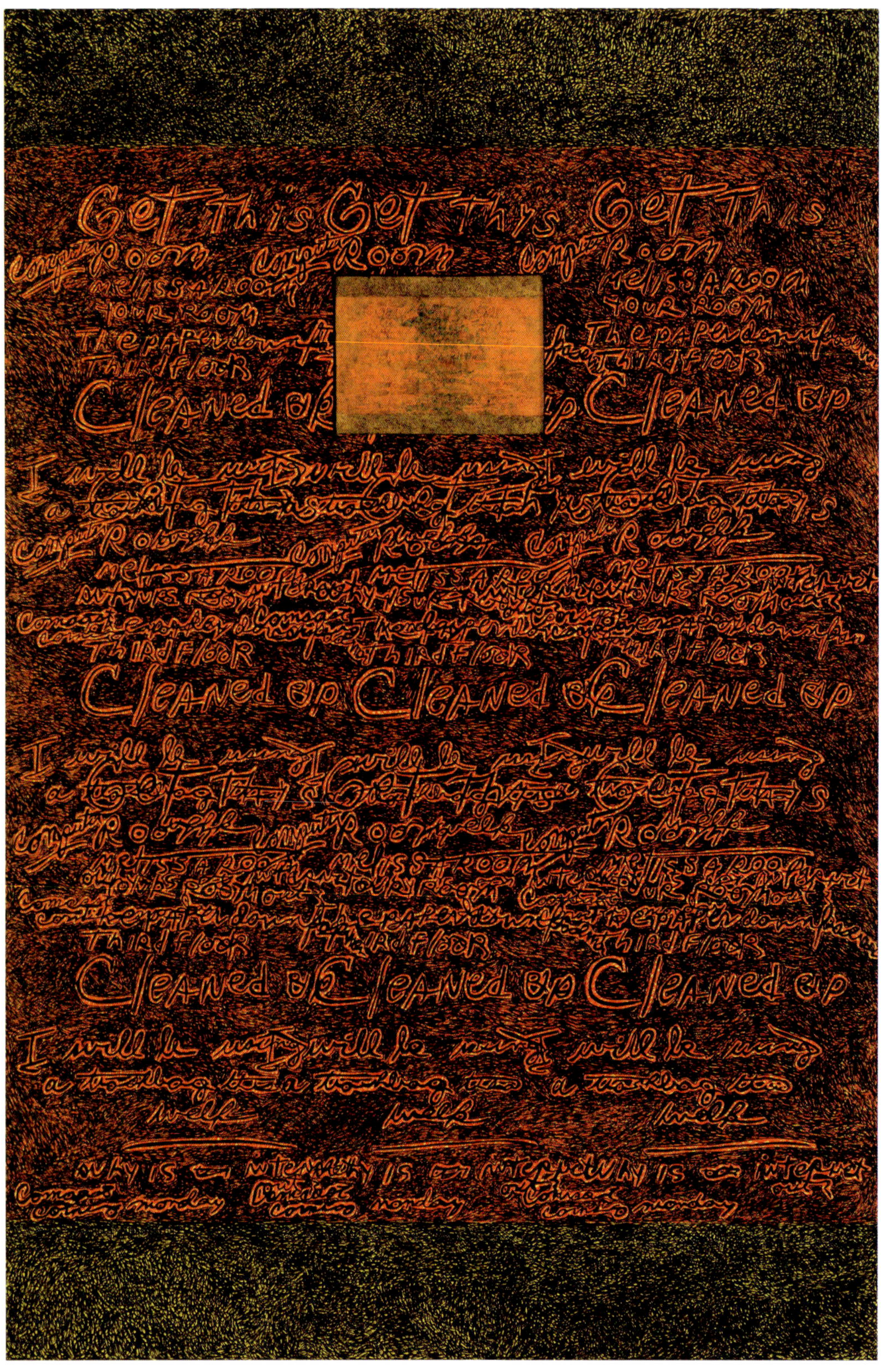
Get This Get This Get This
Computer Room Computer Room Computer Room
YOUR ROOM YOUR ROOM
THIRD FLOOR
Cleaned up Cleaned up
THIRD FLOOR THIRD FLOOR THIRD FLOOR
Cleaned up Cleaned up Cleaned up
Cleaned up Cleaned up Cleaned up
I will be I will be I will be

builds up his drawings in layers, resulting in lush, heavily marked, colorful grounds—for example, *Triple Note from Mother Four Times* (2014; fig. 63) and a related smaller work, *Note from Mother, Versions #1* (2014), in which he inserted a photograph of the actual note his mother had left for him.

In fraktur, Campuzano recognizes "a wonderful sense of invention matched by rigor and design" not dissimilar to his own "mix of improvisation and rules." He also identifies with fraktur's "use of borders and other motifs to guide, constrain, or emphasize the text."[5] Some of Campuzano's compositions suggest individual pages, a double spread, or a book cover—such as *War Path (Philadelphia)* (2008), based on a newspaper clipping from the *Philadelphia Inquirer*, and *Freedom & the Guy*, an homage to the visionary American painter Forrest Bess (1911–1977) in red, yellow, and blue (2005; fig. 64).

FIG. 63 (LEFT)
Anthony Campuzano, *Triple Note from Mother Four Times*, 2014. Ink on paper board, 30 x 20 in.
COURTESY THE ARTIST AND FLESHER/OLLMAN, PHILADELPHIA

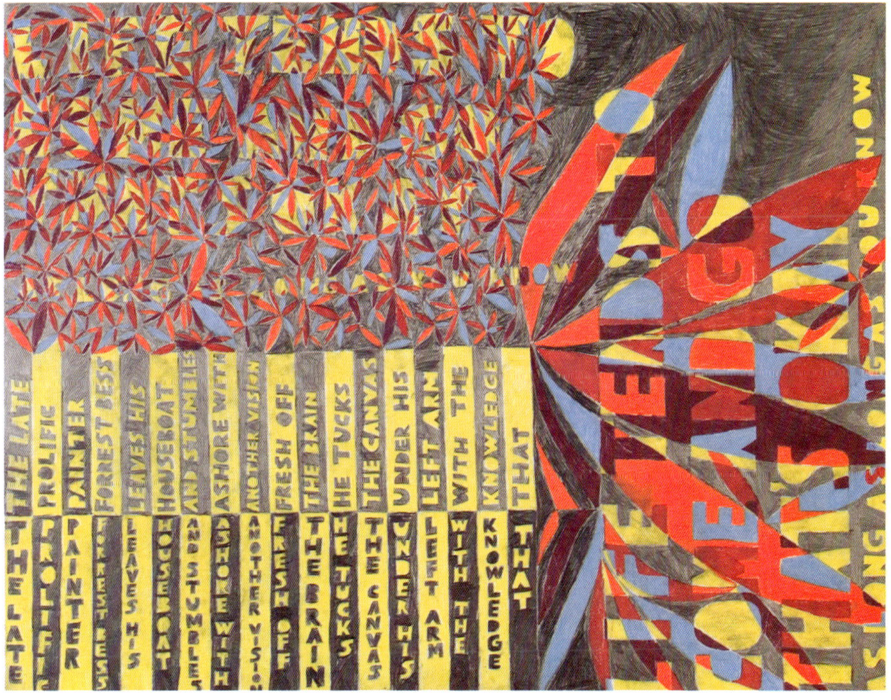

FIG. 64 (BELOW)
Anthony Campuzano, *Freedom & the Guy*, 2005. Colored pencil on illustration board, 30 x 40 in.
COLLECTION ROBERT L. PFANNEBECKER

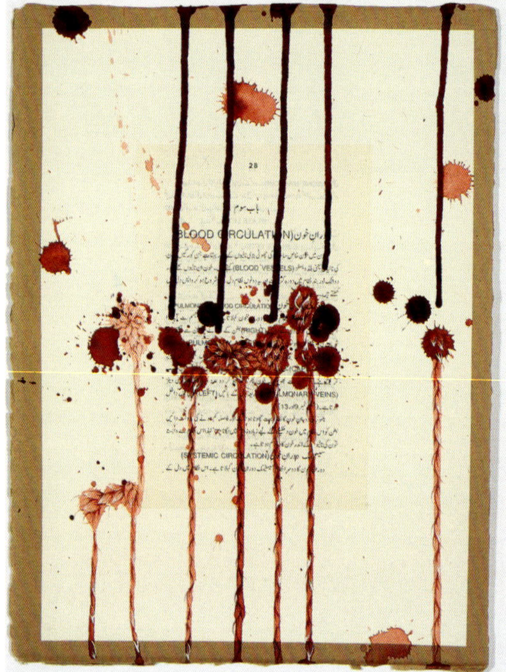

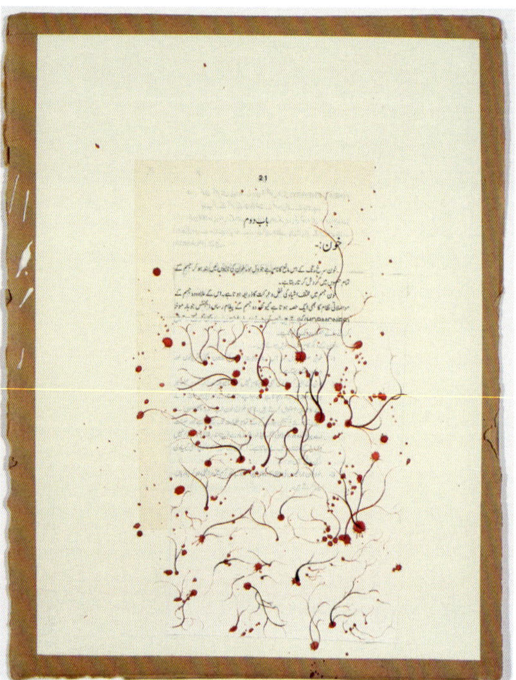

FIG. 65
Imran Qureshi, *Hard to Understand*, 2013. Collage, ink, and gouache on wasli paper, two drawings, 15 x 11⅜ in. each
COURTESY THE ARTIST AND CORVI-MORA, LONDON

Book pages are central to the work of **IMRAN QURESHI** (b. 1972), one of the leading Pakistani artists who integrate the motifs and techniques of traditional miniature painting, which flourished in the Mughal courts of the Indian subcontinent in the late sixteenth century, to develop a contemporary aesthetic. Whereas classical miniature painting was usually limited to religious subjects, court life, and war, Qureshi and his peers use traditional techniques to consider current social and political issues in their region.

Often Qureshi collages and sands pages down so that only some of the words remain readable, creating his own text from the printed page. The printed material in Qureshi's work is in Urdu, considered the most poetic of Pakistan's languages. Deep red paint suggesting blood covers the ground in several recent large-scale outdoor installations, including *The Roof Garden Commission: Imran Qureshi* at the Metropolitan Museum of Art, New York, during summer and fall 2013. From a distance, visitors may think it's a battlefield of spilled blood, but on closer viewing, delicate clusters of petals and flowers become evident. This contrast and tension between refined natural beauty and violence reflecting turbulent

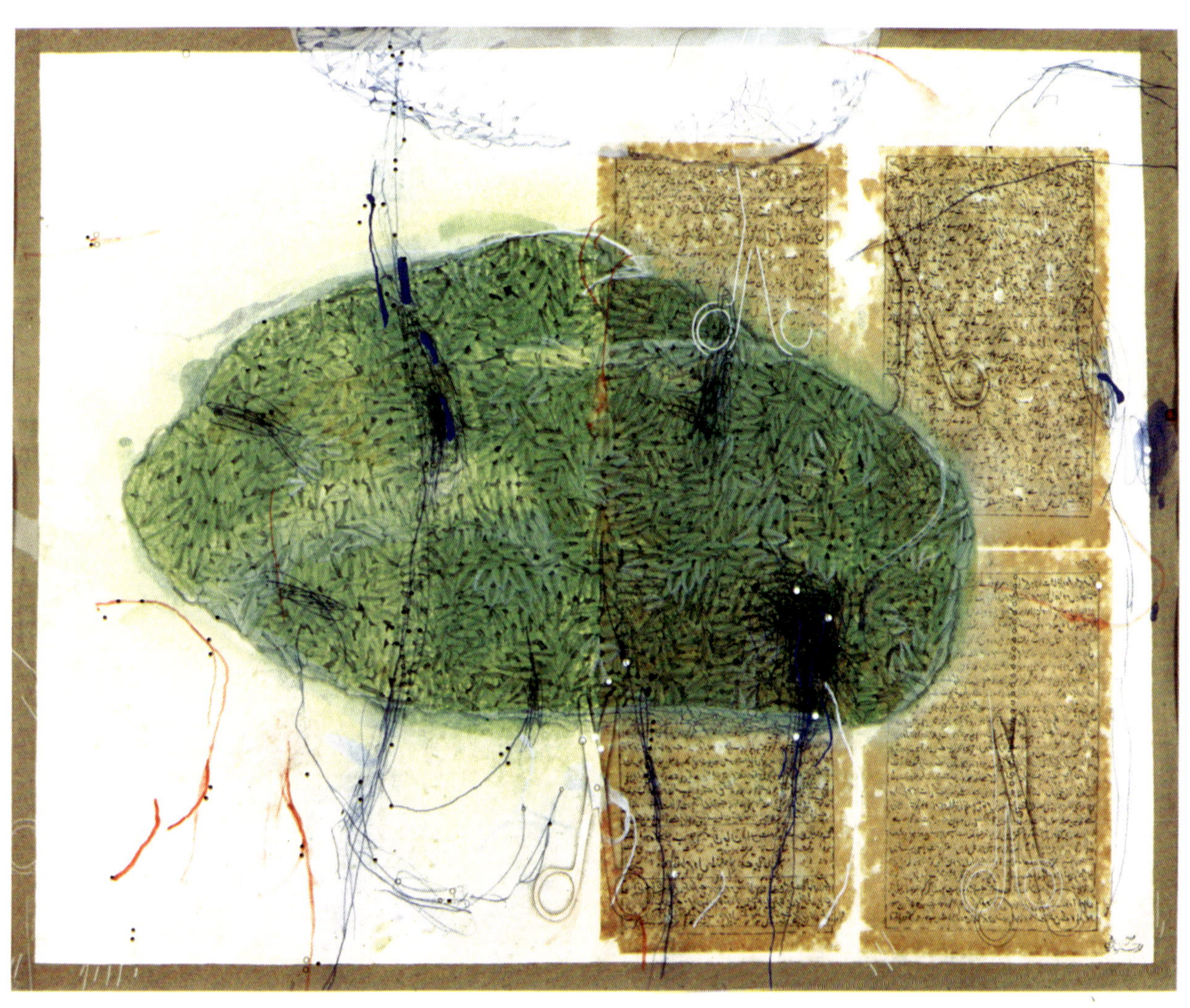

FIG. 66

Imran Qureshi, *Reshape*, 2004. Gouache on wasli paper, 35 x 40⅛ in.

COURTESY THE ARTIST AND CORVI-MORA, LONDON

political conditions in Pakistan also characterize a group of five drawings from 2013 painted on pages from a medical book about the heart and blood circulation. Two are titled *Hard to Understand* (fig. 65) and three *Heart to Understand*. The titles seem to underscore the mystery of the heart: its romantic role as the center of emotions as well as its primal physical function of pumping blood through the body.

ELAINE REICHEK (b. 1943) also explores a rich historic tradition that fuses images with text—the American (and European) embroidered sampler—thereby revealing astute observations about her own time and culture. From the seventeenth to the nineteenth centuries, the needlework sampler was an educational tool used to teach girls their sewing and their letters at the same time. Since the 1980s, Reichek has pioneered a revival of interest in craft techniques and forms associated with women's work, using them to investigate women's narratives and issues affecting marginalized people.

Reichek's contemporary interpretations of traditional samplers relate to fraktur in several ways. Both are folk genres, and both utilize language for its visual qualities (figs. 67, 68). Reichek observes:

> I am particularly drawn to similarities in the ways that fraktur manuscripts and embroideries use decorative alphabets, certainly as a means for conveying particular information, but also for sheer visual effect. Like fraktur manuscripts, many embroideries rely on a vocabulary of related and coded motifs that are arranged in different configurations to generate a variety of decorative patterns. For example, the simplified renderings of trees, houses, and plants in fraktur function like ideograms that, in turn, resemble the charming abstracted style of representation employed in many early samplers.[6]

Among the conventional motifs found in both samplers and fraktur (as well as in the religion and mythology of many cultures) is the "tree of life" or "tree of knowledge" alluding to the creation and interconnection

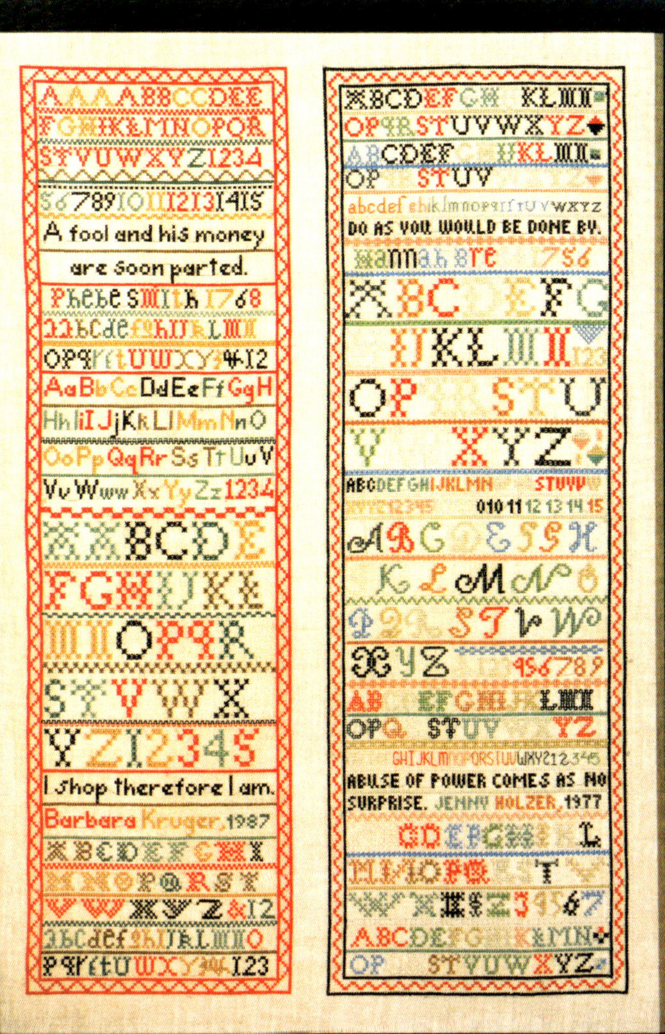

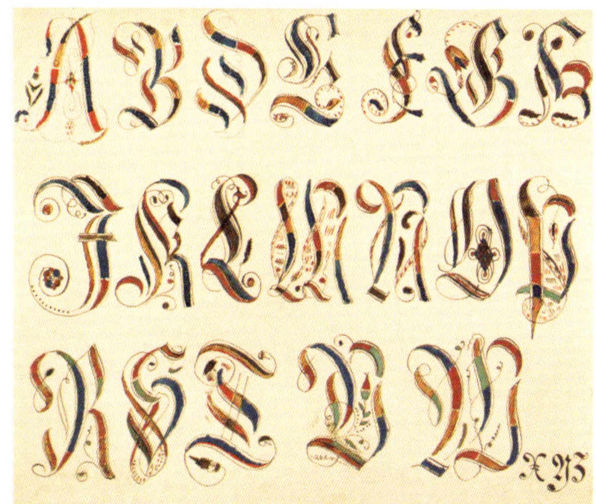

FIG. 67 (LEFT)
Elaine Reichek, *Sampler (Kruger/Holzer)*, 1998. Hand embroidery on linen, 30½ x 21¾ in.
COLLECTION MELVA BUCKSBAUM AND RAYMOND LEARSY

FIG. 68 (ABOVE)
Alphabet. Southeastern Pennsylvania, c. 1800–20. Watercolor and ink on laid paper, 9¼ x 11 in.
FREE LIBRARY OF PHILADELPHIA

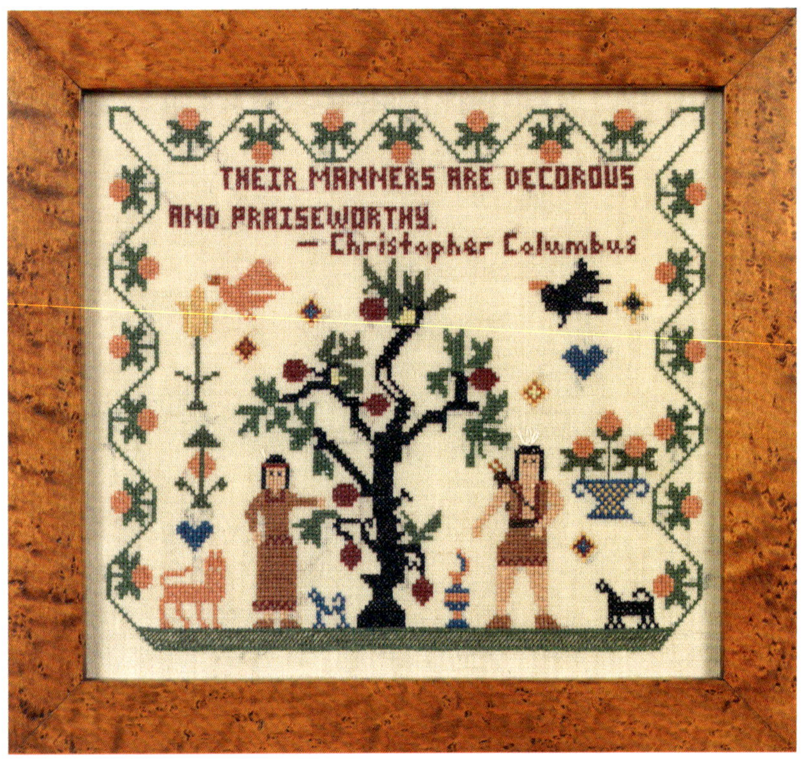

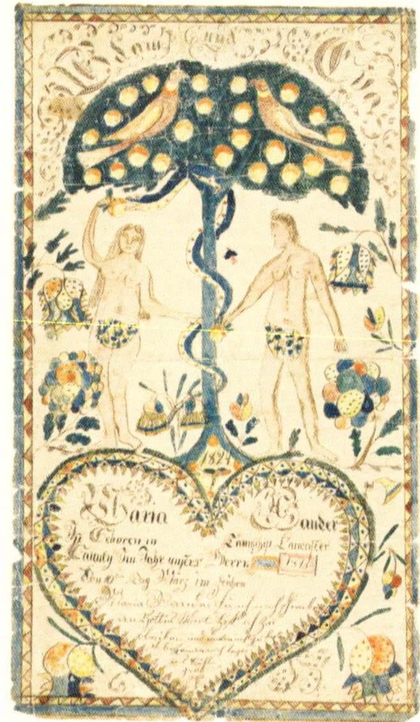

of plant and animal life (fig. 70). Instead of representing the expected figures of Adam and Eve, in *Sampler (Their Manners Are Decorous)* (1992; fig. 69), Reichek shifts the narrative to a Native American couple accompanied by a quotation from Christopher Columbus, thereby reflecting identity politics and multiculturalism that came of age in the 1990s. More than twenty years later, the artist returns to the tree of life theme, this time transforming the composition of Gustav Klimt's 1905–11 Art Nouveau mural into her own needlepoint *Minoan Family Tree* (2014; fig. 71), featuring small cartouches with the names of gods and goddesses in a fraktur-like font arranged in the branches. Tracing "the familial relations between the women of Crete, beginning with Europa, the first mother," Reichek's embroidered composition records the descendants of Greek mythology for a contemporary audience in much the same way as the Pennsylvania German community used fraktur to record their own births, baptisms, marriages, and deaths.[7]

FIG. 69 (ABOVE LEFT)
Elaine Reichek, *Sampler (Their Manners are Decorous)*, 1992. Hand embroidery on linen, 13¼ x 14¾ in.
COURTESY THE ARTIST AND ZACH FEUER GALLERY, NEW YORK

FIG. 70 (ABOVE)
Birth certificate for Maria Xander. Lancaster County, Pennsylvania, 1824. Watercolor and ink on wove paper, 12¾ x 7½ in.
FREE LIBRARY OF PHILADELPHIA

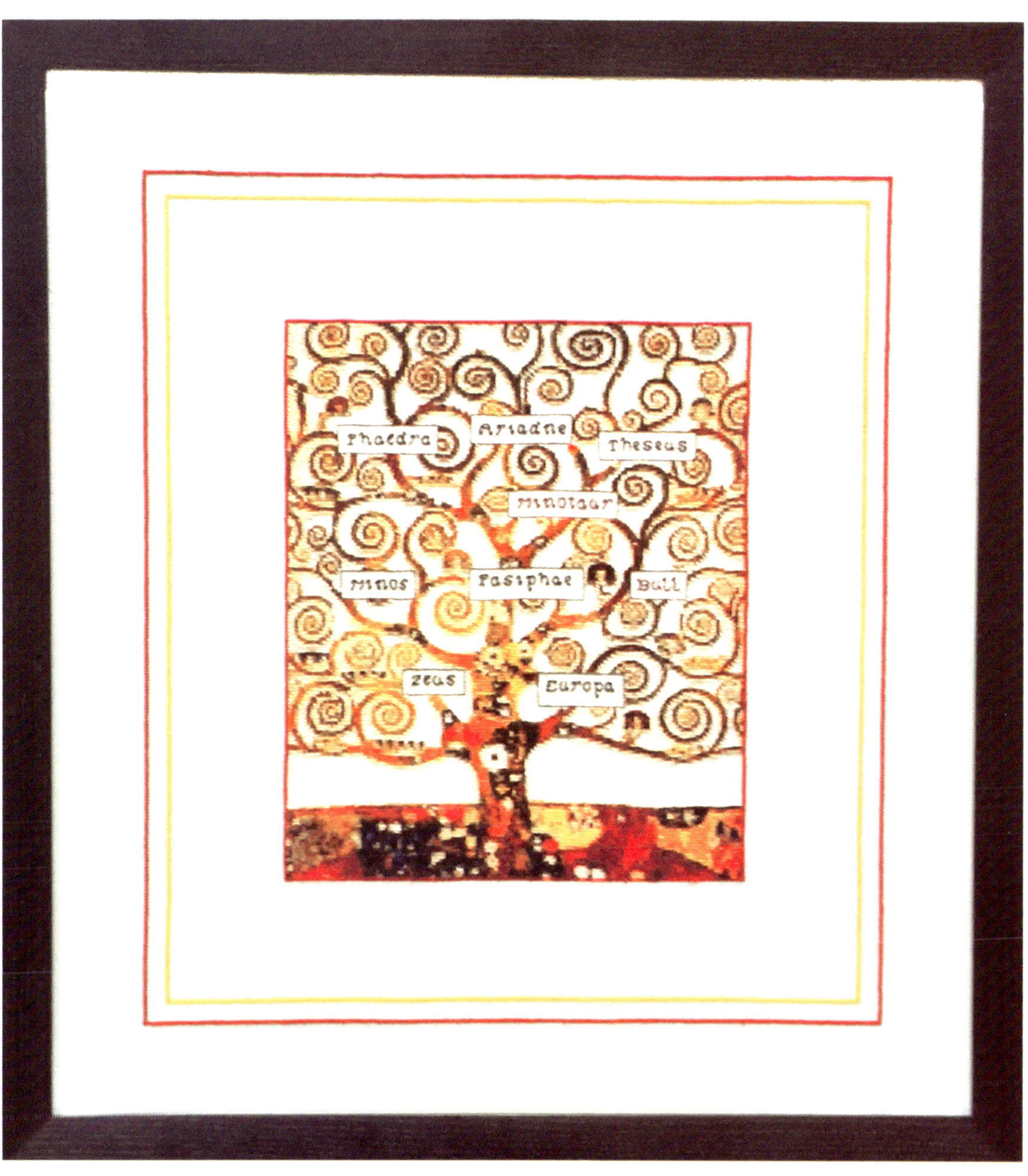

FIG. 71
Elaine Reichek, *Minoan Family Tree*, 2014. Hand embroidery on linen, 24 x 22⅛ in.
COURTESY THE ARTIST AND ZACH FEUER GALLERY, NEW YORK

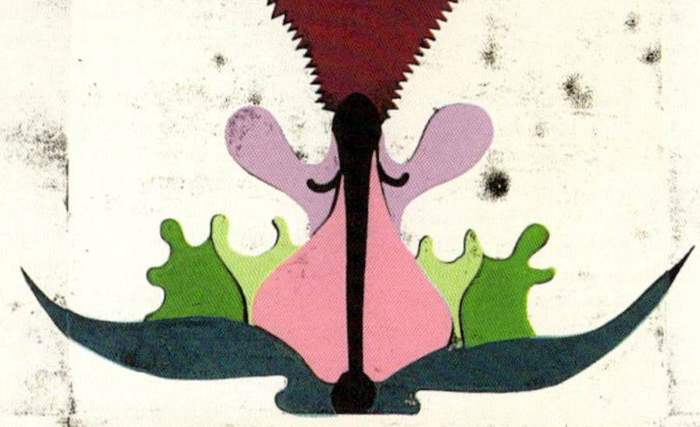

MARCH 2 JUNE 14 2015

WORD & IMAGE

CONTEMPORARY ARTISTS CONNECT TO FRAKTUR

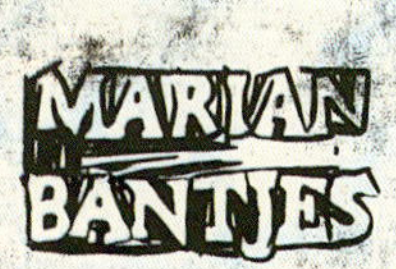

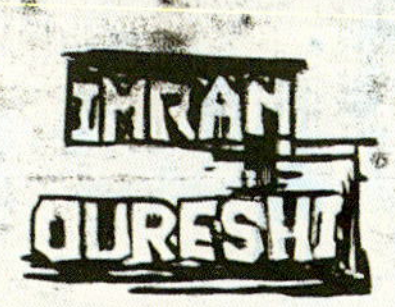

BOB AND ROBERTA
SMITH

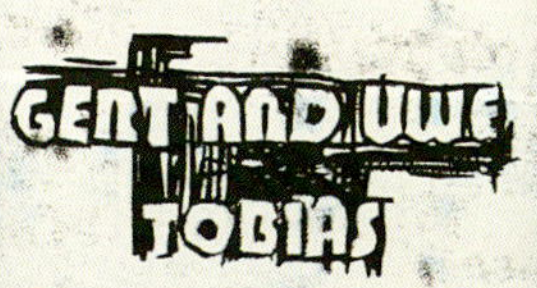

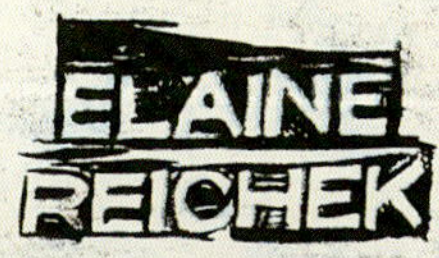

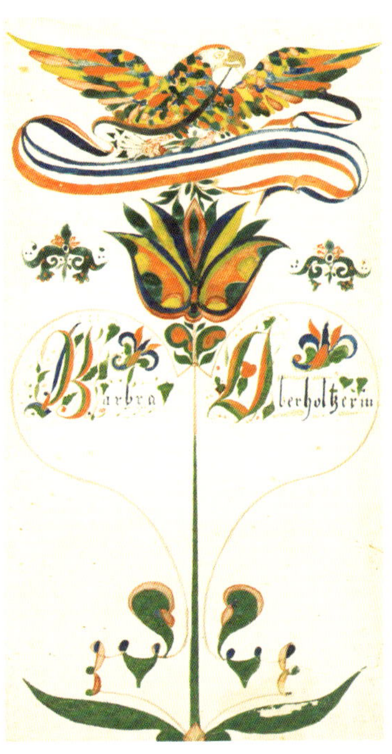

FIG. 72 (LEFT)
Gert and Uwe Tobias, *Untitled*, 2014. Colored woodcut and linotype on paper, $81\frac{1}{8} \times 68\frac{1}{2}$ in.
COURTESY THE ARTISTS AND TEAM GALLERY, NEW YORK

FIG. 73 (ABOVE)
Drawing for Barbra Oberholtzer. Bucks County, Pennsylvania, c. 1840. Watercolor on wove paper, $17\frac{1}{8} \times 8\frac{7}{8}$ in.
FREE LIBRARY OF PHILADELPHIA

GERT AND UWE TOBIAS (b. 1973), twin brothers who create all their work collaboratively, were born in Brasov, Romania, but belong to a German minority there called *Siebenbürger Sachsen* (Transylvanian Saxons). After settling permanently in Germany at the age of twelve with their family, they didn't return to Romania until they were in their twenties. This visit kindled an interest in the folk art and folklore of Transylvania and Eastern Europe that has underpinned their work ever since, combined with their knowledge of early twentieth-century art movements like Constructivism, geometric abstraction, and Surrealism.

Known for large-scale woodblock prints, the Tobiases created an invitation woodcut especially for the exhibition *Word & Image* (2014; fig. 72; see also fig. 75) to announce the show in the library's imposing lobby entrance. The design for this large print is directly related to a c. 1840 drawing in the library's fraktur collection (fig. 73). It features a stylized heart, flower, and leaves as well as an eagle at the top, which the Tobiases chose to eliminate. Between the lobby's grand classical columns, six woodcuts all of the same size and titled *Die Mappe* (the folder), referring to an old collection of embroidery patterns, feature pictographic symbols that merge symbolic language with graphic design (2009; fig. 74; see also fig. 76). The paper is covered with a uniform grid suggesting the background pattern for needlework or weaving. In addition, a large handwoven wool carpet is suspended above the grand staircase, where it can be seen from several vantage points (see figs. 78, 80). The pattern is based on one of the Tobiases' typewriter drawings, a body of work created using an obsolete machine with which they produce a variety of quirky images: some resemble figures, plants, and animals, or architecture as well as textual phrases. The Tobiases seamlessly integrate references to handicraft and folk motifs with art-historical source material spanning from medieval Europe to the twentieth century—an approach that seems decidedly twenty-first century.

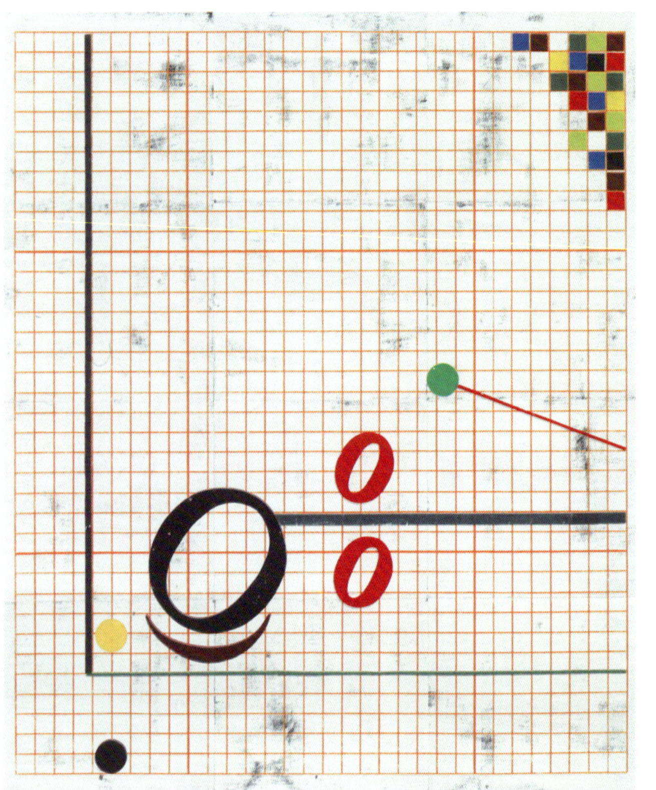

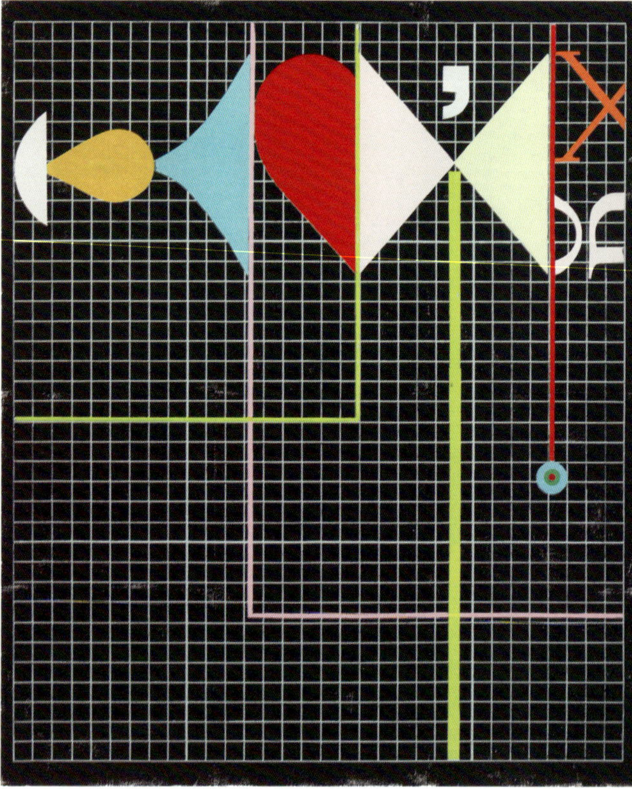

FIG. 74

Gert and Uwe Tobias,
Untitled (Die Mappe), 2009.
Colored woodcuts on
paper, 81⅛ x 68½ in. each

COURTESY THE ARTISTS AND
TEAM GALLERY, NEW YORK

Many other contemporary artists are recognized for exploring the relationship between text and image and experimenting with language as a visual medium—Conceptualist pioneers like Lawrence Weiner, John Baldessari, and Joseph Kosuth; painter Ed Ruscha; Kay Rosen, whose roots are in linguistics; Xu Bing, Glenn Ligon, Paul Chan, and Tauba Auerbach, to name just a few from other generations. The artists featured in *Framing Fraktur* were selected because their work resonates with the look or content of Pennsylvania German fraktur. This is not to say that they are directly influenced by or indebted to fraktur. But it is hoped that the juxtaposition of their new and recent art with the historic folk manuscripts enriches our understanding and appreciation of both. Just as artists today have much to learn from the past, those who study the past may gain insights by considering what artists are doing now. Artists are often ahead of the curve.

NOTES

1 Marian Bantjes's website, www.bantjes.com.

2 Ibid.

3 Bob and Roberta Smith, email to the author, February 2, 2014.

4 Pierogi Gallery press release for *The Art Party (Gotham Golem)*, Bob and Roberta Smith exhibition at The Boiler, November 11–December 22, 2011.

5 Anthony Campuzano, email to the author, January 2, 2015.

6 Elaine Reichek, "Fraktur notes," with email to the author, December 19, 2014.

7 Ibid.

Judith Tannenbaum, a Philadelphia-based curator and writer, retired from her position as Richard Brown Baker Curator of Contemporary Art at the Museum of Art Rhode Island School of Design in 2013. Tannenbaum has organized numerous exhibitions focusing on painting, sculpture, video, and interdisciplinary work, with a particular interest in relationships among fine art, craft, and design.

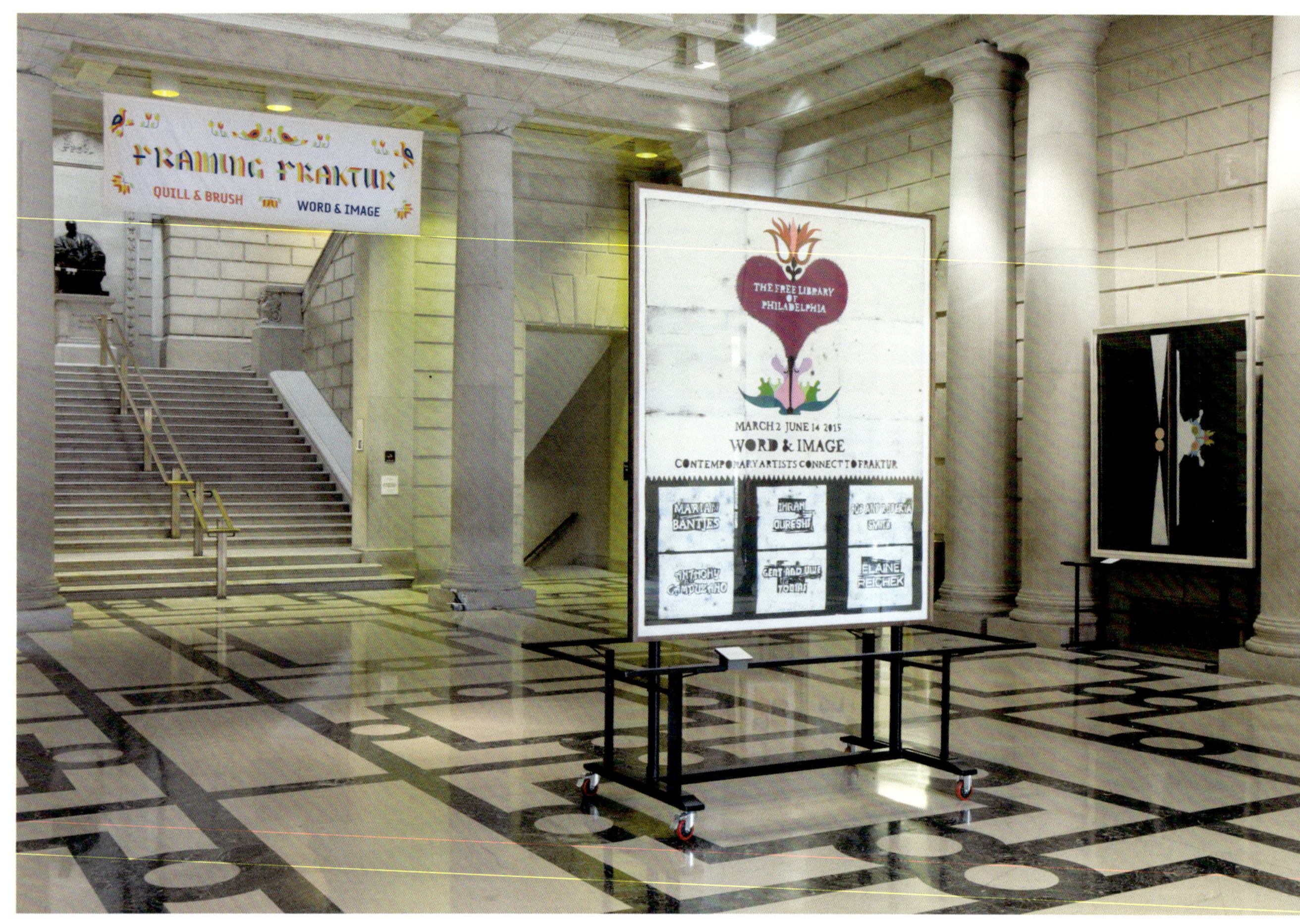

FIG. 75 (ABOVE)
Word & Image installation, library lobby with large-scale woodcuts by Gert and Uwe Tobias. *Untitled*, in the center of the space, was created as an invitation to the exhibition.

FIG. 76 (RIGHT)
Word & Image installation, library lobby with large-scale *Die Mappe* woodcuts by Gert and Uwe Tobias.

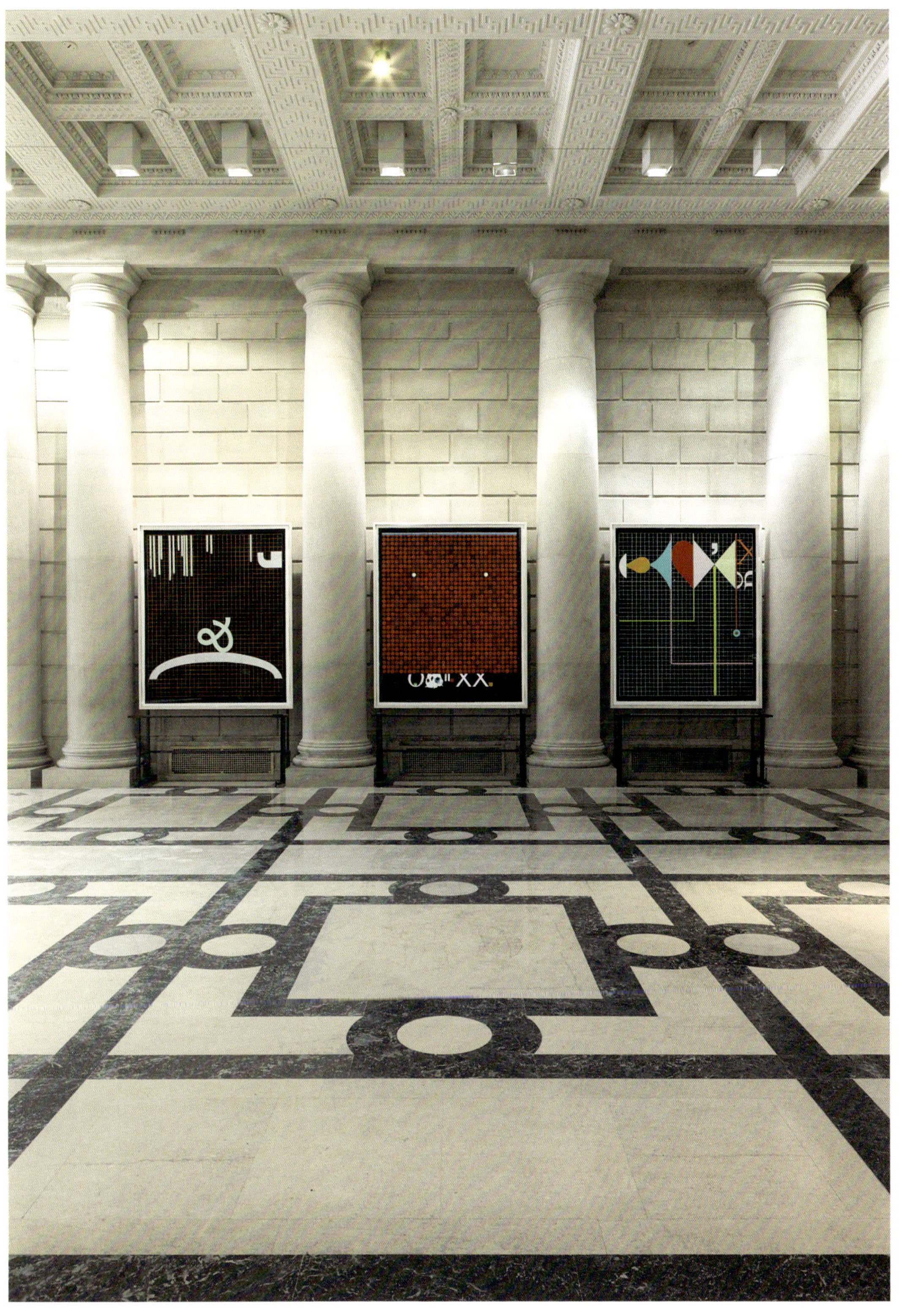

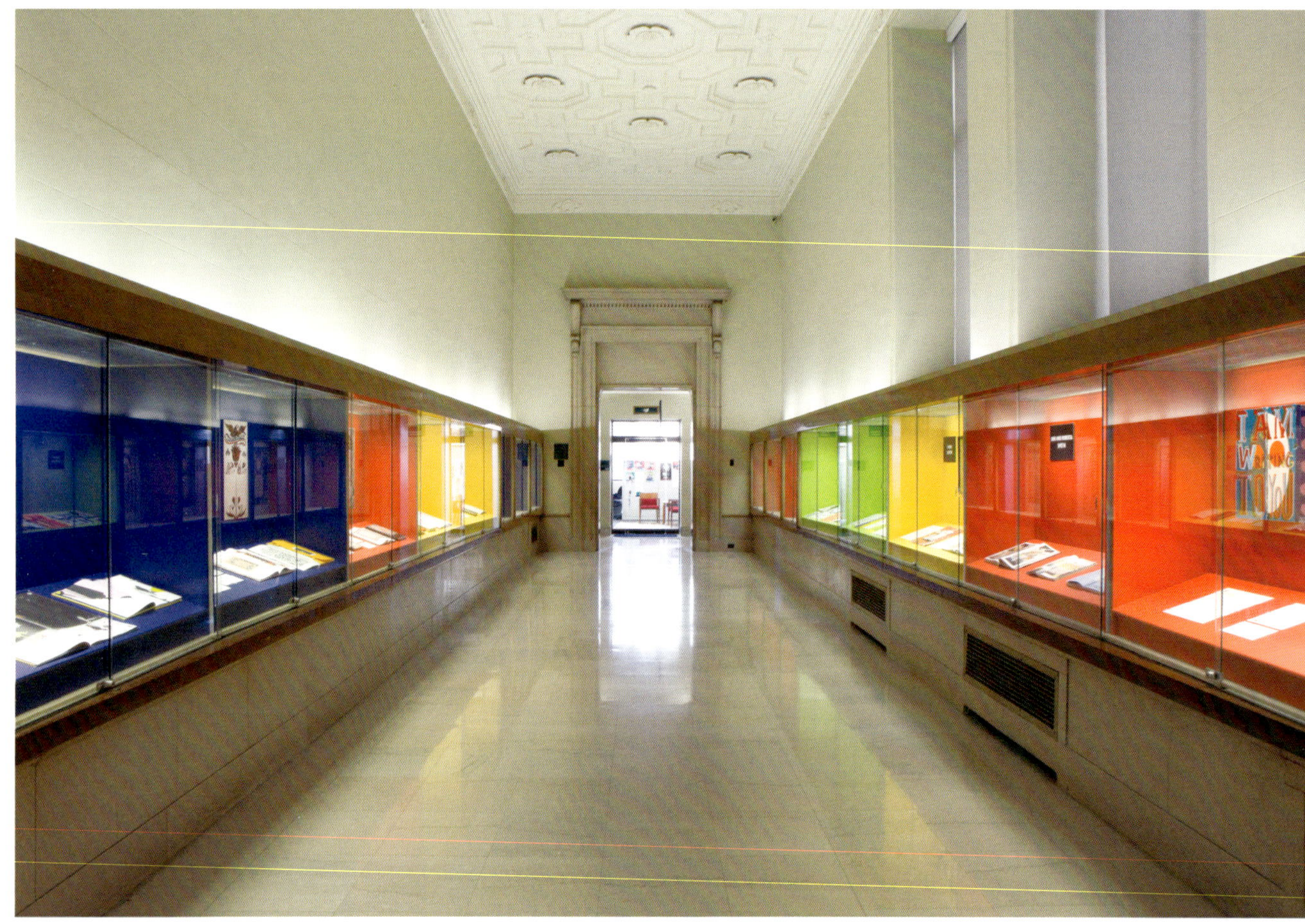

FIG. 77 (ABOVE)
Framing Fraktur installation, first floor gallery with cases introducing contemporary artists with works and publications, juxtaposed with facsimile reproductions of historic fraktur.

FIG. 78 (RIGHT)
Word & Image installation, central staircase with suspended *Untitled* carpet by Gert and Uwe Tobias.

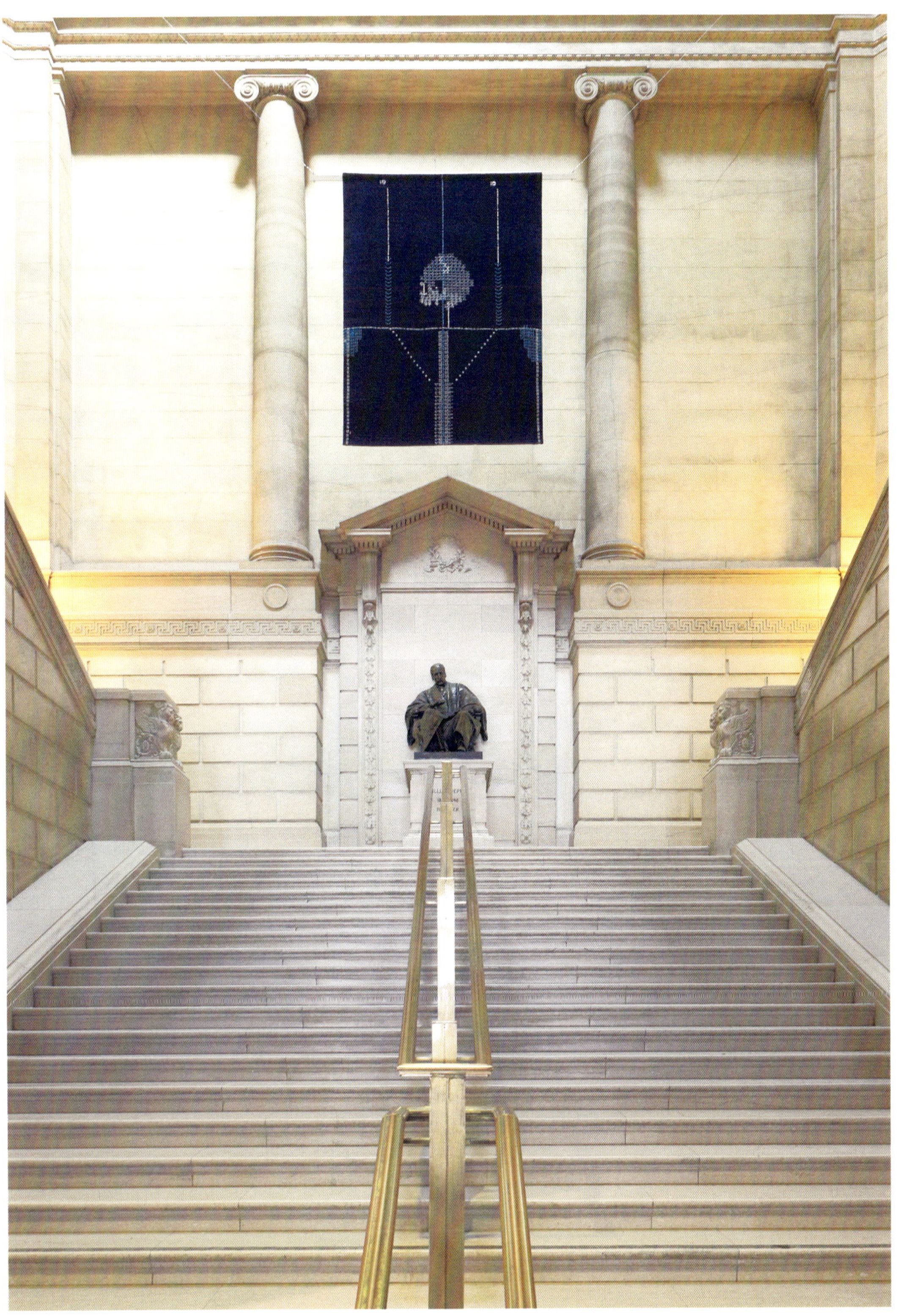

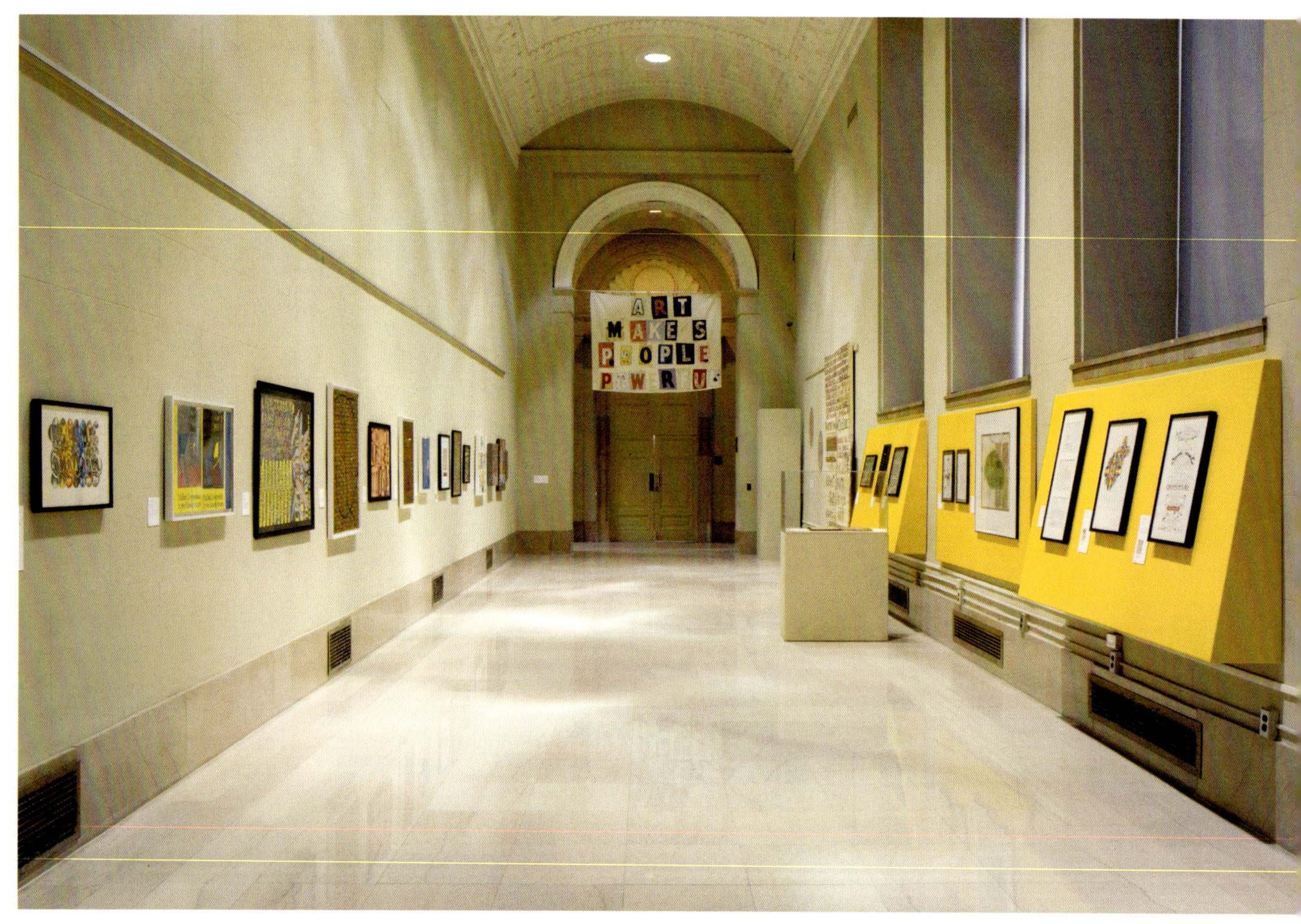

FIG. 79

Word & Image installation, second floor gallery with works by Marian Bantjes, Anthony Campuzano, Imran Qureshi, Elaine Reichek, and Bob and Roberta Smith (including Smith's *Art Makes People Powerful* banner at the end of the gallery).

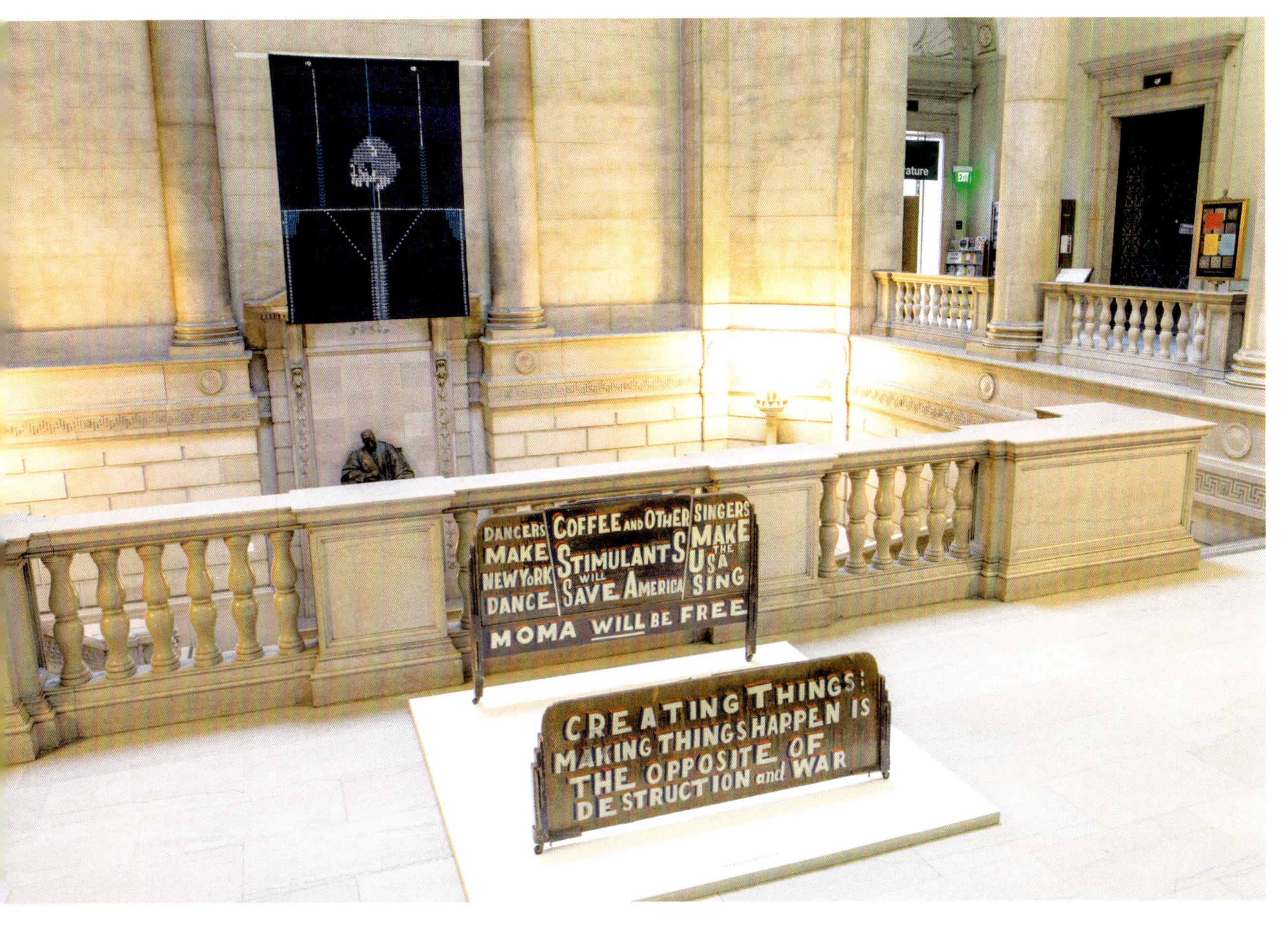

FIG. 80
Word & Image installation, second floor landing with suspended *Untitled* (carpet) by Gert and Uwe Tobias, and *MoMA Will Be Free* (headboard) and *Creating Things* (footboard) by Bob and Roberta Smith.

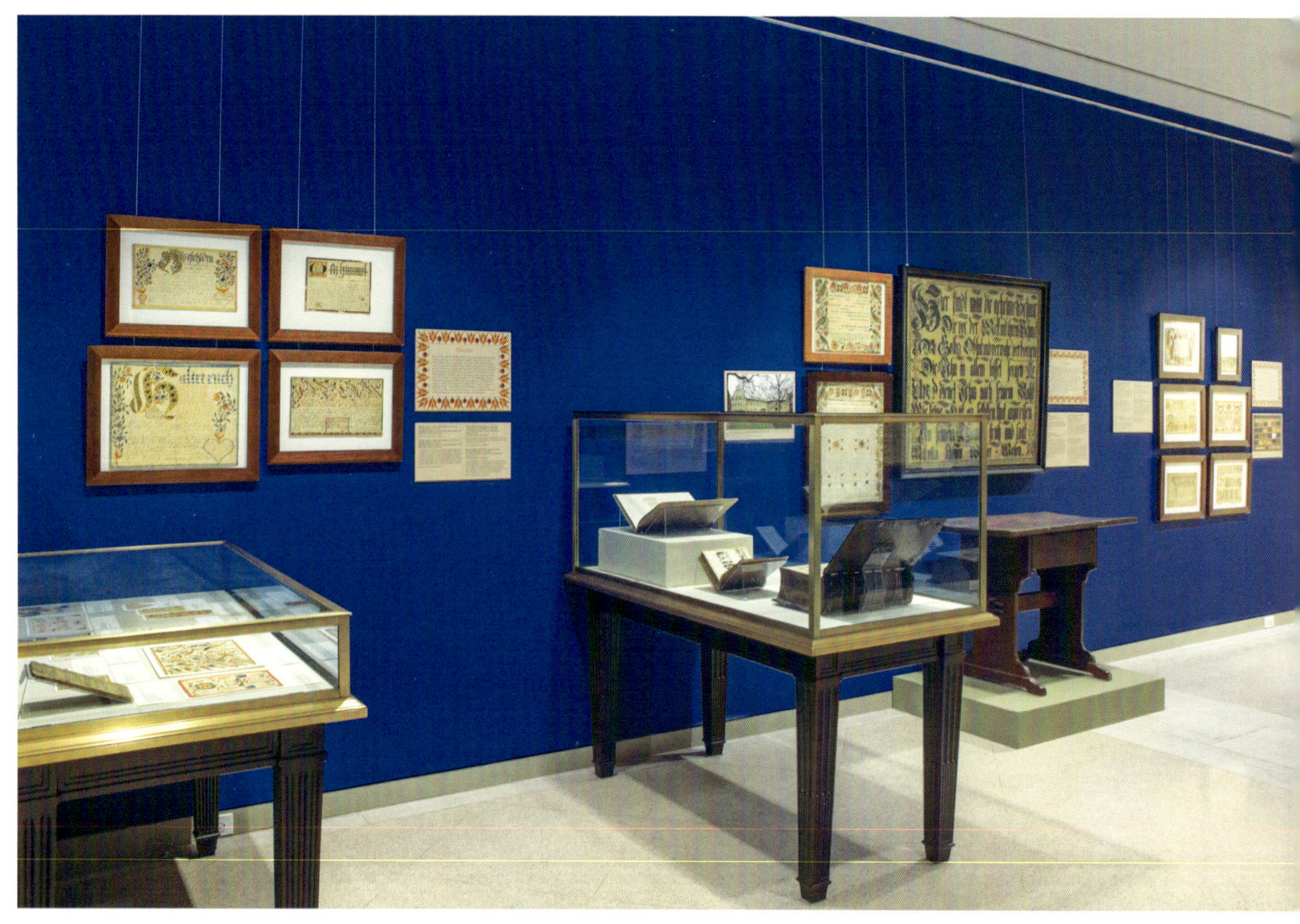

FIG. 81
Quill & Brush installation,
Rare Book Department,
William B. Dietrich Gallery

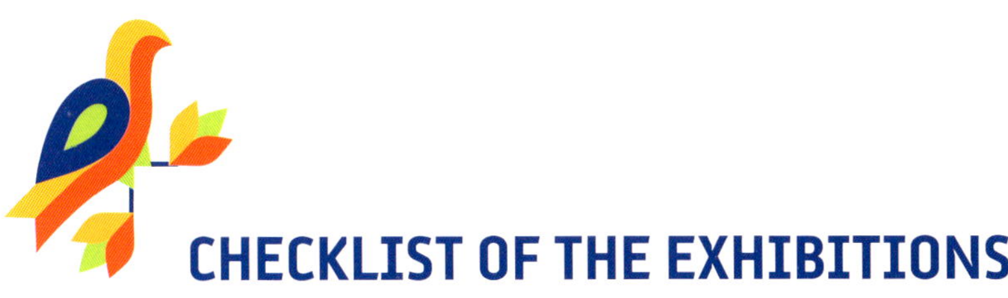

CHECKLIST OF THE EXHIBITIONS

QUILL & BRUSH
Pennsylvania German Fraktur and Material Culture

Artists and/or printers are named when the object is firmly documented with a signature, initials, or imprint. When no such documentation exists but there is strong evidence to support an attribution, the phrase "attributed to" is used. Less-firm attributions are designated as "probably by" or "possibly by." Where applicable, location changes caused by the formation of new townships or counties are also noted. Materials were identified through visual examination. Dimensions are overall, height followed by width, and do not include the frame unless otherwise noted. FRK numbers refer to the Free Library of Philadelphia's comprehensive digital database, available at www.freelibrary.org/fraktur. All objects belong to the Rare Book Department unless otherwise noted.

MAKING FRAKTUR

Alphabet

Southeastern Pennsylvania, c. 1800–20. Watercolor and ink on laid paper, 9¼ × 11 in.

FRK00026 **FIG. 68**

Box with fraktur

Probably Lehigh County, Pennsylvania; c. 1830–50. Pine, watercolor, ink, laid and wove paper, 4⅝ × 10 × 8¼ in.

Artist's tool kit

Southeastern Pennsylvania, c. 1800. Leather, iron; bone, brass, glass; watercolor, ink, laid paper, 2 × 4¾ × 2½ in.

FRKR00001 **FIG. 4**

Birth, baptismal, and confirmation certificate for Friedrich Hill

Attributed to the Wetzel-Geometric Artist, Richmond Township, Berks County, Pennsylvania, c. 1816. Watercolor and ink on laid paper, 7¾ × 13⅛ in.

FRK00645

Woodblock

Northampton-Lehigh County area, Pennsylvania, c. 1800. Pine, 13 × 15¼ × 1 in.

FRKR00002 **FIG. 6**

Birth and baptismal certificate for Salomon Zimmerman

Attributed to the Flying Angel Artist (active 1780–1811), Lowhill Township, Northampton (now Lehigh) County, Pennsylvania, c. 1811. Watercolor and ink on laid paper, 13 × 15¾ in.

FRK00085

Account book with bookplate for Johannes Funck

Attributed to Johannes Ernst Spangenberg (c. 1755–1814), Northampton County, Pennsylvania, 1789. Watercolor and ink on laid paper, 12¼ × 8¼ in.

FRKB01032 **FIG. 11**

Birth and baptismal certificate for Elisabetha Wollfinger

Attributed to Johann Adam Eyer (1755–1837), Northampton (now Monroe) County, Pennsylvania, c. 1801. Ink and watercolor on laid paper, 10 × 8 in.

FRK00376 **FIG. 12**

Birth and baptismal certificate for Elisabetha Eyer

Attributed to Johann Adam Eyer (1755–1837), Northampton (now Monroe) County, Pennsylvania, c. 1802. Watercolor and ink on laid paper, 10 × 8 in.

FRK00377 **FIG. 13**

Religious text

Attributed to Johann Adam Eyer (1755–1837), Bucks County, Pennsylvania, 1782. Watercolor and ink on laid paper, 8 × 6⅝ in.

FRK00541

Cutwork picture for Elisabeth Detweiler

Attributed to Wilhelm Antonius Faber (active 1790–1820), Berks County, Pennsylvania, 1826. Watercolor and ink on wove paper, 6¼ × 3⅝ in.

FRK00657

Religious text

Attributed to Samuel Gottschall (1808–1898), Franconia Township, Montgomery County, Pennsylvania, 1833. Watercolor and ink on wove paper, 7¾ × 12⅝ in.

FRK00644 **FIG. 21**

Birth and baptismal certificate for Phillip Jacob Kohr

Decoration attributed to Conrad Gilbert (1734–1812), Berks County, Pennsylvania, c. 1785. Watercolor and ink on laid paper, 8⅜ × 13¼ in.

FRK00400

New Year's Wish

Christian Mertel (1739–1802), Mount Joy Township, Lancaster County, Pennsylvania, 1796. Watercolor and ink on laid paper, 7¾ × 13 in.

FRK00170

Letter H

Attributed to Susanna Heebner (1750–1818), Worcester Township, Montgomery County, Pennsylvania, c. 1810. Watercolor and ink on laid paper, 8¼ × 6⅝ in.

FRK00652 **FIG. 1**

Birth and baptismal certificate for Isaac Lantz

Attributed to Friedrich Krebs (1749–1815), Williams Township, Northampton County, Pennsylvania, c. 1792. Watercolor and ink on laid paper, 7⅞ × 13 in.

FRK01097

EPHRATA

Writing table

Attributed to the Ephrata Cloister, Ephrata, Lancaster County, Pennsylvania, c. 1750. Walnut, tulip poplar, pine, 29 × 38 × 23 in.

ROCKY HILL COLLECTION

Religious text

Attributed to the Ephrata Cloister, Ephrata, Lancaster County, Pennsylvania, c. 1750. Ink on leather, 34 × 37½ in.

COLLECTION OF JOSEPH B. SHELANSKI

Paradisisches Wunder-Spiel

Printed and decorated by the Ephrata Cloister, Ephrata, Lancaster County, Pennsylvania, 1754. Watercolor and ink on laid paper, 13 × 8 in.

FRKM114000 **FIG. 14**

Tune book

Attributed to the Snow Hill Cloister, Quincy, Franklin County, Pennsylvania, c. 1820–40. Watercolor and ink on wove paper, 3½ × 7¼ in.

FRK0115201

Hymnal with bookplate for Hermann Zinn

Attributed to the Ephrata Cloister, Ephrata, Lancaster County, Pennsylvania, c. 1750. Watercolor and ink on laid paper, 7⅜ × 10¾ in.

FRKB00080

Der Blutige Schau-Platz oder Märtyrer Spiegel

Printed by the Ephrata Cloister, Ephrata, Lancaster County, Pennsylvania, 1748. Ink on laid paper; leather, wood, brass, 14½ × 10¼ in.

Religious text

Attributed to the Ephrata Cloister, Ephrata, Lancaster County, Pennsylvania, c. 1750. Ink and watercolor on laid paper, 7 × 8⅝ in.

FRK00710

Birth and baptismal certificate for Barbara Miller

Decoration after Henrich Otto (1733–c. 1799), printing attributed to the Ephrata Cloister, Ephrata, Lancaster County, Pennsylvania, c. 1785. Watercolor and ink on laid paper, 12⅞ × 15¾ in.

FRK00004 **FIG. 18**

Spiritual Labyrinth

Decoration attributed to Henrich Otto (1733–c. 1799), printing attributed to the Ephrata Cloister, Ephrata, Lancaster County, Pennsylvania, 1785. Watercolor and ink on laid paper, 20⅞ × 16⅛ in.

FRK01057

RELIGION

Bible

Printed by Christopher Saur Sr. (1693–1758), Germantown, Pennsylvania, 1743. Ink on laid paper; leather, wood, brass, 10½ × 8¼ in.

Der Frommen Lotterie

Written by Gerhard Tersteegen (1697–1769), possibly printed by Christopher Saur Sr. (1695–1758), Germantown, Pennsylvania; c. 1744. Leather; ink on laid paper, 4⅜ × 4⅛ × 2⅝ in.

Religious text

Attributed to Conrad Gilbert (1734–1812), Berks County, Pennsylvania, c. 1800. Watercolor and ink on laid paper, 6¾ × 3½ in.

FRK00619

Drawing of a pelican in her piety

Attributed to David Kulp (1777–1834), Bucks County, Pennsylvania, c. 1820. Watercolor and ink on wove paper, 5 × 3 in.

FRK00584

Religious text

Attributed to Johannes Mayer (active 1769–1812), Bucks County, Pennsylvania, c. 1800. Watercolor and ink on laid paper, 5 × 3 in.

FRK00625

Marriage blessing for Christian Meyer and Maria Landes

Johann Adam Eyer (1755–1837), Bedminster Township, Bucks County, Pennsylvania, 1784. Watercolor and ink on laid paper, 10 × 7⅞ in.

FRK00636

Drawing of a comet

Attributed to Daniel Schumacher (d. 1787), probably Berks County, Pennsylvania; c. 1769. Watercolor and ink on laid paper, 7 × 11⅝ in.

FRK00696

Wunderfisch

Southeastern Pennsylvania, c. 1820. Watercolor and ink on wove paper, 7¾ × 13⅛ in.

FRK00317

Drawing of Christ preaching to his disciples

Attributed to Durs Rudy Sr. (1766–1843) or Durs Rudy Jr. (1789–1850), Lehigh County, Pennsylvania, c. 1820–40. Watercolor and ink on wove paper, 8¾ × 6⅝ in.

FRK00309 **FIG. 20**

Religious text

Bucks or Montgomery County, Pennsylvania, April 4, 1817. Watercolor and ink on laid paper, 15⅞ × 13 in.

FRK00714 **FIG. 58**

Religious text

Attributed to Susanna Heebner (1750–1818), Worcester Township, Montgomery County, Pennsylvania, August 22, 1807. Watercolor and ink on laid paper, 8 × 13¼ in.

FRK00635 **FIG. 22**

Religious text

Probably Lancaster County, Pennsylvania; c. 1785. Watercolor and ink on laid paper, 13 × 16 in.

FRK00071

Religious text

Attributed to Christian Beschler (active 1796–c. 1815), Upper Mahanoy Township, Northumberland County, Pennsylvania, February 19, 1799. Watercolor and ink on laid paper, 12 × 15 in.

FRK00721

Adam und Eva, im Paradies

Printed by Carl A. Bruckmann (1792–1828), Reading, Berks County, Pennsylvania, c. 1820. Watercolor and ink on laid paper, 15⅞ × 12⅝ in.

FRKS00003

Tall clock

Movement by George Hoff (1733–1816), Lancaster, Pennsylvania, c. 1790. Walnut, oak; brass, iron, bronze, steel; glass, 96 × 20 × 12 in.

Spiritual clockworks for Johannes Burckhardt

Attributed to John William Bernthausel (active c. 1785–1815), Berks County, Pennsylvania, 1815. Watercolor and ink on laid paper, 6¼ × 8 in.

FRK00653

BIRTH & BAPTISM

Letter from the godparents

Alsace, France, 1815. Watercolor and ink on laid paper with pinpricking, 8⅜ × 9½ in.

FRK01119 **FIG. 15**

Baptismal wish for Eva Eissenhaer

Attributed to the Sussel-Washington Artist (active c. 1760–85), Bethel Township, Lancaster (now Lebanon) County, Pennsylvania, c. 1773. Watercolor and ink on laid paper, 6½ × 7⅞ in.

FRK00681 **FIG. 16**

Birth and baptismal certificate for Maria Elisabeth Müller

Henrich Otto (1733–c. 1799), Millbach area, Lebanon County, Pennsylvania, c. 1775. Watercolor and ink on laid paper, 12¾ × 16¼ in.

FRK00053 **FIG. 17**

Birth and baptismal certificate for Georg Glück

Attributed to Conrad Trevits (1751–1830), Heidelberg Township, Dauphin (now Lebanon) County, Pennsylvania, c. 1812. Watercolor and ink on laid paper, 12⅝ × 16 in.

FRK00009

Birth and baptismal certificate for Johannes Dinges

Attributed to Christian Mertel (1739–1802), Lebanon Township, Dauphin (now Lebanon) County, Pennsylvania, c. 1796. Watercolor and ink on laid paper, 12⅝ × 15 in.

FRK00740

Birth and baptismal certificate for Elisabetha Zeyber

Decoration and infill attributed to Friedrich Speyer (active c. 1774–1801), Heidelberg Township, Lancaster (now Lebanon) County, Pennsylvania, c. 1790. Watercolor and ink on laid paper, 13⅛ × 16 in.

FRK01001

Birth and baptismal certificate for Anna Maria Krum

Attributed to Karl Münch (1769–1833), Schaefferstown, Dauphin (now Lebanon) County, Pennsylvania, c. 1800. Watercolor and ink on laid paper, 12⅝ × 15 in.

FRK00711

Birth and baptismal certificate for Elisabeth Lindaman

Attributed to the Northampton County Artist, Allen Township, Northampton County, Pennsylvania, c. 1820. Watercolor and ink on wove paper, 15⅞ × 12 in.

FRK00039

Birth and baptismal certificate for Elisabeth Kauffman

Attributed to the Oley Township Artist (active 1799–1828), Maidencreek Township, Berks County, Pennsylvania, 1825. Watercolor and ink on wove paper, 10 × 7⅞ in.

FRK00685

Birth and baptismal certificate for Susanna Clementine Fisher

Philadelphia, Pennsylvania, c. 1808. Watercolor and ink on laid paper, 12¾ × 15½ in.

FRK00717 **FIG. 19**

Birth certificate for Catherine Styre

Attributed to Samuel Bentz (1792–1850), Lancaster County, Pennsylvania, c. 1835. Watercolor and ink on wove paper, 10 × 8 in.

FRK00676

Birth and baptismal certificate for Maria Frey

Martin Brechall (c. 1757–1831), Lowhill Township, Northampton (now Lehigh) County, Pennsylvania, November 25, 1813. Watercolor and ink on laid paper, 10⅞ × 17⅛ in.

FRK00115

Birth, baptismal, and confirmation certificate for Elisabeth Scheffi

Johann Valentin Unger, Limerick Township, Montgomery County, Pennsylvania, c. 1800. Watercolor and ink on laid paper, 12 × 15 in.

FRK00731

Birth and baptismal certificate for Benedict Gerber

Attributed to the Soly Deo Gloria Artist, New Providence Township, Montgomery County, Pennsylvania, c. 1797. Watercolor and ink on laid paper, 7⅞ × 12½ in.

FRK00364

Birth and baptismal certificate for Lewaina Bähr

Johannes Renninger, Colebrookdale Township, Berks County, Pennsylvania, 1841. Watercolor and ink on wove paper, 16⅜ × 13 in.

FRK00005

Birth and baptismal certificate for Sara Anna Utz

Daniel Peterman (1797–1871), Manheim Township, York County, Pennsylvania, c. 1838. Watercolor and ink on wove paper, 12½ × 16 in.

FRK00069

EDUCATION

Eine Einfältige und gründliche abgefaßte Schul-Ordnung

Written by Christopher Dock (d. 1771), printed by Christopher Saur Jr. (1721–1784), Germantown, Pennsylvania, 1770. Ink on laid paper, 7⅝ × 5 in.

Reward of merit (heart)

Southeastern Pennsylvania, c. 1800. Watercolor and ink on laid paper, 3⅝ × 3⅜ in.

FRK00241

Reward of merit for Susanna Scheuer

Attributed to Martin Brechall (c. 1757–1831), Lehigh County, Pennsylvania, December 3, 1811. Watercolor and ink on laid paper, 7⅞ × 6½ in.

FRK00469 **FIG. 24**

Reward of merit (drawing of flowers)

Attributed to the Engraver Artist, southeastern Pennsylvania, c. 1800. Watercolor and ink on laid paper, 4⅛ × 3⅜ in.

FRK00602

Reward of merit (circle of heads)

Bucks or Montgomery County, Pennsylvania, c. 1820. Watercolor and ink on wove paper, 5 × 3 in.

FRK00241A

Reward of merit (drawing of flowers)

Southeastern Pennsylvania, c. 1820. Watercolor and ink on wove paper, 7⅝ × 6⅜ in.

FRK00715 **FIG. 5**

Drawing of birds and a schoolmaster

School of Johann Adam Eyer (1755–1837), probably Bucks County, Pennsylvania; March 10, 1816. Watercolor and ink on laid paper, 8 × 13⅜ in.

FRK00631

Reward of merit (drawing of a priest)

Probably Bucks or Montgomery County, Pennsylvania; c. 1820. Watercolor and ink on wove paper, 5½ × 3⅜ in.

FRK00723

Reward of merit (drawing of an angel)

Attributed to Johann Adam Eyer (1755–1837), probably Bucks County, Pennsylvania; c. 1790. Watercolor and ink on laid paper, 2⅝ × 3⅜ in.

FRK00564

Reward of merit (drawing of a deer)

Attributed to Johann Adam Eyer (1755–1837), probably Bucks County, Pennsylvania; c. 1790. Watercolor and ink on laid paper, 4⅛ × 3¾ in.

FRK01089

Drawing for Dina Kriebel

Montgomery County, Pennsylvania, 1843. Watercolor and ink on wove paper, 5¾ × 10⅛ in.

FRK00548

Reward of merit (drawing of a flower)

Attributed to David Kriebel (1787–1848), Gwynedd Township, Montgomery County, Pennsylvania, c. 1800. Watercolor and ink on laid paper, 3¾ × 2⅞ in.

FRK00651

Reward of merit (drawing of a flower)

Attributed to David Kulp (1777–1834), Bucks County, Pennsylvania, c. 1800. Watercolor and ink on laid paper, 6⅞ × 2⅝ in.

FRK00591

Drawing of a bird for Sarah Ebersol

Attributed to Barbara Ebersol (1846–1922), Lancaster County, Pennsylvania, 1869. Watercolor and ink on wove paper, 8⅜ × 7 in.

FRK00425

Writing sample for David Herr

Hans Jacob Brubacher (c. 1730–1802), Providence Township, Lancaster County, Pennsylvania, January 23, 1766. Watercolor and ink on laid paper, 7 × 9⅛ in.

FRK00550 **FIG. 25**

Writing sample booklet with bookplate for Abraham Landes

Attributed to Johann Adam Eyer (1755–1837), Perkasie School, Hilltown Township, Bucks County, Pennsylvania, May 25, 1780. Watercolor and ink on laid paper, 8⅜ × 6⅜ in.

FRK00716 **FIG. 10**

Writing sample for Ester Hadmänn

Attributed to Johann Adam Eyer (1755–1837), Bucks County, Pennsylvania, c. 1790. Watercolor and ink on laid paper,
8 × 12⅞ in.

FRK00347

Writing sample for Michael Musselmann

Christian Strenge (1757–1828), Hempfield Township, Lancaster County, Pennsylvania, 1794. Watercolor and ink on laid paper, 12⅝ × 15½ in.

FRK00713 **FIG. 7**

Writing sample for Michael Musselmann

Christian Strenge (1757–1828), Hempfield Township, Lancaster County, Pennsylvania, 1795. Watercolor and ink on laid paper, 7¾ × 12⅞ in.

FRK00637

Writing sample for Anna Scherg

Attributed to Christian Alsdorff (c. 1760–1838), Earl Township, Lancaster County, Pennsylvania, January 10, 1800. Watercolor and ink on laid paper, 7¾ × 13 in.

FRK00370 **FIG. 26**

MUSIC

Tune book with bookplate for Henrich Honsperger

Attributed to Johann Adam Eyer (1755–1837), Perkasie School, Hilltown Township, Bucks County, Pennsylvania, April 12, 1780. Watercolor and ink on laid paper, 4 × 6½ in.

FRKB00013

Tune book with bookplate for Jacob Hunsicker

Attributed to Johann Adam Eyer (1755–1837), Perkasie School, Hilltown Township, Bucks County, Pennsylvania, January 29, 1783. Watercolor and ink on laid paper, 4 × 6½ in.

FRKB01037

Hymnal with bookplate for Peter Miller

Attributed to Johann Adam Eyer (1755–1837), Vincent Township, Chester County, Pennsylvania, May 21, 1789. Watercolor and ink on laid paper, 6½ × 4 in.

FRKB00091

Hymnal with bookplate for David Kolb

Attributed to Johann Adam Eyer (1755–1837), Deep Run School, Bedminster Township, Bucks County, Pennsylvania, May 8, 1783. Watercolor and ink on laid paper, 5⅞ × 3¼ in.

FRKB01058 **FIG. 28**

Hymnal with embossed cover

Printed by Heinrich Ludwig Brönner, Marburg or Frankfurt, Germany, 1785. Leather, brass, watercolor, ink, laid paper, 6 × 3½ in.

Hymnal with bookplate for Esther Kolb

Attributed to David Kulp (1777–1834), Bucks County, Pennsylvania, December 27, 1813. Watercolor and ink on laid paper, 6½ × 3⅞ in.

FRKB00104

Catechism with bookplate for Anna Landes

Attributed to David Kulp (1777–1834), Bedminster Township, Bucks County, Pennsylvania, May 22, 1803. Watercolor and ink on laid paper, 5¼ × 3⅛ in.

FRKB01022 **FIG. 29**

Tune book with bookplate for Anna Lädtermänn

Attributed to David Kulp (1777–1834), Deep Run School, Bucks County, Pennsylvania, January 12, 1812. Watercolor and ink on wove paper, 3¾ × 6⅜ in.

FRKB01036

Tune book with bookplate for Ludwig Beck

Attributed to Johann Adam Eyer (1755–1837), Upper Mount Bethel School, Northampton County, Pennsylvania, March 2, 1797. Watercolor and ink on laid paper, 4 × 6⅝ in.

FRKB00007 **FIG. 27**

Tune book with bookplate for Elisabeth Christman

Upper Milford Township, Lehigh County, Pennsylvania, c. 1820. Watercolor and ink on wove paper, 4⅛ × 7¾ in.

FRKB01017

Tune book with bookplate for Rossina Reinwalt

Probably Bucks County, Pennsylvania; October 15, 1792. Watercolor and ink on laid paper, 4 × 6⅝ in.

FRKB00001

FOOD & MEDICINE

Die Geschickte Hausfrau

Printed by Johann Martin Lutz and Theodore Scheffer, Harrisburg, Pennsylvania, 1848. Ink on wove paper, 6¼ × 4¼ in.

Die Wahre Brantewein Brennerey, oder, Brantwein, Gin, und Cordialmacher Kunst, wie auch die ächte Färbe Kunst

Printed by Salomon Mäyer, York, Pennsylvania, 1797. Ink on laid paper, 6 × 4 in.

Die Land- und Haus-Apotheke, oder getreuer und gründlicher Unterricht für den Bauer und Stadtmann

Printed by Carl A. Bruckmann (1792–1828), Reading, Berks County, Pennsylvania, 1818. Ink on laid paper; leather, 7 × 4¼ in.

Dish

Southeastern Pennsylvania, c. 1800–50. Lead-glazed earthenware (redware), 9 × 9 × 1 in.

Gingerbread mold owned by Christopher Ludwig (1720–1801)

Probably Philadelphia, Pennsylvania; c. 1760–75. Fruitwood, 3⅝ × 6¾ × 1⅜ in

MUSEUM OF THE AMERICAN REVOLUTION

Der Hoch-Deutsche Americanische Calendar

Printed by Michael Billmeyer (1752–1837), Germantown, Pennsylvania, 1803. Ink on laid paper, 8½ × 7 in.

Box of powwow formulas

Southeastern Pennsylvania, c. 1850–1900. Wallpaper, paper board, wove paper, ink, 7½ × 9 × 1½ in.

Box of powwow formulas

Southeastern Pennsylvania, c. 1850–1900. Tinned sheet iron, wove paper, ink, 6 × 8 × 1 in.

WEAVING

Weaver's draft book of Peter Leisey (1802–1859)

Cocalico Township, Lancaster County, Pennsylvania, 1816. Ink and watercolor on laid paper, 4 × 6½ in.

FRKM079000

Weaver's draft book of Johann Philip Meyer (d. 1825)

Kutztown, Berks County, Pennsylvania, 1794. Watercolor and ink on laid paper, 8 × 6½ in.

FRKM077000

Weaver's draft book of Peter Diller

York County, Pennsylvania, 1839. Ink on wove paper, 7⅞ × 6½ in.

FRKM076000

Weaver's pattern book

Southeastern Pennsylvania, c. 1800. Watercolor and ink on laid paper, 8 × 7 in.

FRKM075000

Coverlet

Peter Leisey (1802–1859), Cocalico Township, Lancaster County, Pennsylvania, c. 1840. Wool and cotton weft with a cotton warp, 95 × 72 in

PRIVATE COLLECTION

Length of cloth

Probably Pennsylvania; c. 1800–50. Linen, 67⅝ × 16⅞ in.

BEYOND SOUTHEASTERN PENNSYLVANIA

Birth and baptismal certificate for Elisabeth Miller

John George Busyaeger (1774–1843), Westmoreland County, Pennsylvania, 1839. Watercolor and ink on wove paper, 12⅛ × 15⅜ in.

FRK01253

Birth and baptismal certificate for Martha Burger

Attributed to George Burger (1790–1861), Franklin Township, Westmoreland County, Pennsylvania, c. 1846. Watercolor and ink on wove paper, 16⅜ × 13⅛ in.

FRK01100

New Year's Wish

Attributed to Johann Carl Scheibeler, probably Westmoreland County, Pennsylvania; 1798. Watercolor and ink on laid paper, 7⅝ × 6⅜ in.

FRK00523

Birth certificate for Johanna Flori

David Cordier (active c. 1805–20), Montgomery County, Ohio, 1815. Ink on laid paper, 7¾ × 12⅞ in.

FRK00363 **FIG. 30**

Birth and baptismal certificate for Anna Linn

Attributed to Friedrich Bandel (active c. 1800–20), probably Ohio; 1818. Watercolor and ink on wove paper, 12 × 15 in.

FRK01098

Birth and baptismal certificate for Maria Erb

Isaac Ziegler Hunsicker (1803–1870), Waterloo Region, Ontario, Canada, 1836. Watercolor and ink on wove paper, 9⅛ × 7⅝ in.

FRK01046

Birth and baptismal certificate for Margretha Benss

Decoration and infill by Peter Bernhardt (active 1794–1819), printing attributed to Ambrose Henkel (1786–1870), Rockingham County, Virginia, 1814. Watercolor and ink on laid paper, 8 × 13⅛ in.

FRK01104

Birth and baptismal certificate for Helehna Henkel

Attributed to J. G. Cropth (active c. 1800–10), Shenandoah County, Virginia, c. 1801. Watercolor and ink on laid paper, 7¾ × 13⅛ in.

FRK01034

Birth and baptismal certificate for Rosina Banawitz

Attributed to William Weaver, probably Shenandoah County, Virginia; c. 1800. Watercolor and ink on laid paper, 12¼ × 15⅜ in.

FRK00093

WORD & IMAGE
Contemporary Artists Connect to Fraktur

MARIAN BANTJES

Canadian, b. 1963; lives on Bowen Island, British Columbia

Seduction 2006

Custom lettering on poster designed by Michael Bierut, Pentagram. Vector art, 34 × 22 in.

COURTESY THE ARTIST

My Dear, Can We Work Together 2007

Pen and ink on paper, 22½ × 15 in.

COURTESY THE ARTIST

FIG. 57

Tamsin Certificate 2009

Pen and ink on paper, 15 × 11 in.

COLLECTION TAMSIN MILEY

BACK COVER

Localism 2012

Ink and pencil crayon on paper, 22¼ × 15 in.

COURTESY THE ARTIST

Framing Fraktur 2014

Three studies for *Framing Fraktur*. Pencil on paper, 8½ × 11 in. each

COURTESY THE ARTIST

Lost Child 2014

Needlepoint with synthetic hair from My Little Pony figures, 18 × 20 in.

COURTESY THE ARTIST

FIG. 59

Birds (Fraktur) 2015

Ink on watercolor paper, 15 × 22 in.

COURTESY THE ARTIST

Danger: Modernist Fraktur 2015

Ink on watercolor paper, 22 × 15 in.

COURTESY THE ARTIST

Pennsylvania Fraktur Pattern 2015

Watercolor and pencil crayon on watercolor paper, 22 × 15 in.

COURTESY THE ARTIST

FIG. 55

ANTHONY CAMPUZANO

American, b. 1975; lives in Philadelphia

Autobiography: Emily Dickinson via Frances Farmer 2004

Mixed media on paper, 17 × 14 in.

COLLECTION ROBERT L. PFANNEBECKER

Constant Life Crisis 2005

Ink and graphite on graph board, 22 × 28 in.

COLLECTION ROBERT L. PFANNEBECKER

Freedom & the Guy 2005

Colored pencil on illustration board, 30 × 40 in.

COLLECTION ROBERT L. PFANNEBECKER

FIG. 64

War Path (Philadelphia) 2008

Colored pencil, ink, and graphite on board, 20 × 30 in.

COLLECTION BENJAMIN MULVEY

He Is the Greatest Dancer (Portrait of Taylor Mead) 2013

Ink and graphite on paper board, 40 × 30 in.

PRIVATE COLLECTION

Triple Note from Mother Four Times 2014

Ink on paper board, 30 × 20 in.

COURTESY THE ARTIST AND FLEISHER/OLLMAN, PHILADELPHIA

FIG. 63

Note from Mother, Versions #1 2014

Ink and colored pencil with inset photo on paper board, 20 × 16 in.

COURTESY THE ARTIST AND FLEISHER/OLLMAN, PHILADELPHIA

IMRAN QURESHI

Pakistani, b. 1972; lives in Lahore

Untitled 2001

Gouache and collage on tea-stained wasli paper (book), 13¾ × 11 in. (closed)

COURTESY THE ARTIST AND CORVI-MORA, LONDON

Untitled 2001

Gouache and collage on wasli paper, 16⅞ × 14 in.

COURTESY THE ARTIST AND CORVI-MORA, LONDON

Reshape 2004

Gouache on wasli paper, 35 × 40⅛ in.

COURTESY THE ARTIST AND CORVI-MORA, LONDON

FIG. 66

Hard to Understand 2013

Collage, ink, and gouache on wasli paper, two drawings, 15 × 11⅜ in. each

COURTESY THE ARTIST AND CORVI-MORA, LONDON

FIG. 65

ELAINE REICHEK

American, b. 1943; lives in New York

Sampler (Their Manners Are Decorous) 1992

Hand embroidery on linen, 13¼ × 14¾ in.

COURTESY THE ARTIST AND ZACH FEUER GALLERY, NEW YORK

FIG. 69

Sampler (Dispositional Hypnoid States) 1996

Hand embroidery on linen, 18¾ × 20¼ in.

COLLECTION MELVA BUCKSBAUM AND RAYMOND LEARSY

Sampler (Kruger/Holzer) 1998

Hand embroidery on linen, 30½ × 21¾ in.

COLLECTION MELVA BUCKSBAUM AND RAYMOND LEARSY

FIG. 67

Sampler (Spot Sampler) 1999

Hand embroidery on linen, 18¼ × 16¼ in.

COLLECTION NICOLE KLAGSBRUN

Sampler (Simplicity) 1999

Hand embroidery on linen, 14 × 22 in.

COURTESY THE ARTIST AND ZACH FEUER GALLERY, NEW YORK

White Magic (Enochian Alphabet) 2004

Hand embroidery on linen, 21¼ × 11¼ in.

COURTESY THE ARTIST AND ZACH FEUER GALLERY, NEW YORK

Minoan Family Tree 2014

Hand embroidery on linen, 24 × 22¼ in.

COURTESY THE ARTIST AND ZACH FEUER GALLERY, NEW YORK

FIG. 71

BOB & ROBERTA SMITH (a.k.a. Patrick Brill)

British, b. 1963; lives in London

Pot Eight Toe 2002

Enamel on wood, 32 × 32 × 2 in.

COURTESY THE ARTIST

Will You Make It as an Artist? 2009

Enamel on wood, 31 × 28 × 2 in.

COURTESY THE ARTIST

Art, Music, Poetry 2011

Enamel on found metal (cookie sheet), 18 × 11½ × 1 in.

COURTESY THE ARTIST AND PIEROGI GALLERY

Creating Things 2011

Enamel on found wood (footboard), 57 × 19½ × 1 in.

COURTESY THE ARTIST AND PIEROGI GALLERY

FIG. 80

MoMA Will Be Free 2011

Enamel on found wood (headboard), 56 × 26 × 2 in.

COURTESY THE ARTIST AND PIEROGI GALLERY

FIG. 80

The Museum of Modern Art 2011

Enamel on found paper, 25 × 18½ in. (oval)

COURTESY THE ARTIST AND PIEROGI GALLERY

FIG. 60

No One Owns Art 2011

Enamel on found paper, 25 × 18½ in. (oval)

COURTESY THE ARTIST AND PIEROGI GALLERY

FIG. 60

Give a Child Pencils 2012

Enamel on wood, 24 × 24 × 3 in.

COURTESY THE ARTIST

I Am Writing to You 2012

Enamel on wood, 16 × 14 × 3 in.

COURTESY THE ARTIST

Picasso's Speech to the 1950 Peace Congress 2012

Oil on found wood, 90 × 86¾ in.

COURTESY THE ARTIST

FIG. 61

Art Makes People Powerful 2013

Fabric with appliqué and embroidery (banner), 66 × 91 in.

COURTESY THE ARTIST AND PIEROGI GALLERY

FIGS. 62, 79

GERT & UWE TOBIAS

German, b. 1973; live in Cologne

Untitled (Die Mappe) 2009, 2010, 2011

Six colored woodcuts on paper, 81⅛ × 68½ in. each

COURTESY THE ARTISTS AND TEAM GALLERY, NEW YORK

FIGS. 74–76

Untitled 2014

Wool carpet, approx. 134 × 90 in.

COURTESY THE ARTISTS AND TEAM GALLERY, NEW YORK

FIGS. 78, 80

Untitled 2014

Colored woodcut and linotype on paper, 81⅛ × 68½ in.

COURTESY THE ARTISTS AND TEAM GALLERY, NEW YORK

FIGS. 72, 75

Framing Fraktur: Pennsylvania German Material Culture & Contemporary Art is published in conjunction with two exhibitions presented by the Free Library of Philadelphia:
Quill & Brush: Pennsylvania German Fraktur and Material Culture, March 2 – July 18, 2015
Word & Image: Contemporary Artists Connect to Fraktur, March 2 – June 14, 2015

1901 Vine Street, Philadelphia, Pennsylvania 19103
215-686-5322 / freelibrary.org

Editor: Judith Tannenbaum
Designer: Julie Fry
Copyeditor: Nell McClister
Printing: Studley Press, Dalton, MA
Binding: AcmeBinding, Charlestown, MA
Distribution: University of Pennsylvania Press

Exhibition photography by Greenhouse Media (pp. 6, 72–73, 88, 90, 92–94) and Alistair Overbruck (pp. 88, 91); all other images provided by artist or artist's gallery

Back cover: Love letter for Katharina Martin. Upper Otterbach, Rhine-Palatinate, Germany, 1809. Watercolor and ink on laid paper, 14 in. diameter (FREE LIBRARY OF PHILADELPHIA); Marian Bantjes, *Tamsin Certificate*, 2009. Pen and ink on paper, 15 × 11 in. (COLLECTION TAMSIN MILEY)

Library of Congress Control No. 2015939328
ISBN 978-0-8122-4745-9

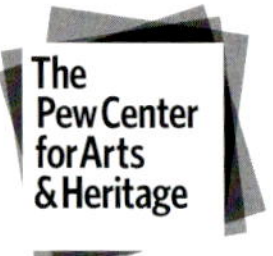

Major support for *Framing Fraktur* has been provided by The Pew Center for Arts & Heritage, with additional support from the Wyeth Foundation for American Art, American Airlines Cargo, Christie's, The Gladys Krieble Delmas Foundation, and the Virginia Cretella Mars Foundation.

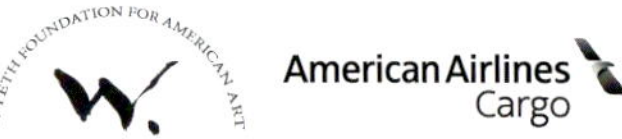

CHRISTIE'S

The Gladys Krieble Delmas Foundation